Green Finance and Investment

Environmental Lending in EU Eastern Partnership Countries

Please cite this publication as:
OECD (2016), *Environmental Lending in EU Eastern Partnership Countries*, Green Finance and Investment, OECD Publishing, Paris.
http://dx.doi.org/10.1787/9789264252189-en

ISBN 978-92-64-25217-2 (print)
ISBN 978-92-64-25218-9 (PDF)

Series: Green Finance and Investment
ISSN 2409-0336 (print)
ISSN 2409-0344 (online)

Revised version, April 2016
Details of revisions available at: *http://www.oecd.org/about/publishing/Corrigendum-EnvironmentalLending.pdf*

Photo credits: Cover © mika48/Shutterstock.com.

Corrigenda to OECD publications may be found on line at: *www.oecd.org/about/publishing/corrigenda.htm*.

Foreword

In the European Union's Eastern Partnership (EaP) countries – Armenia, Azerbaijan, Belarus, Georgia, Moldova and Ukraine – credit lines supported by International Finance Institutions (IFIs) are the main source of long-term funding for green investments, particularly in energy and resource efficiency. It is now 10 years since the design work began on the first IFI credit lines in the region. Learning from the experience with the implementation of such credit lines provides useful insight into the main challenges to increasing the capacity of the EaP banking sector to finance green investment projects.

This report is a background paper supporting a wider OECD project which aims to analyse the conditions that would enable commercial banks in the EaP countries to support environmental investments. Commercial banks have a potentially important role to play in providing lending for green investments. However, under the current conditions in the EaP countries, banks' involvement remains limited. Generally, commercial banks have only established specific environmental credit lines when supported by IFIs and only a small number continue to offer such products once IFI support is withdrawn.

The current report provides an overview of the main environment-related credit lines issued by IFIs, donors and multilateral finance mechanisms and disbursed through local commercial banks in the EaP countries. Where appropriate, examples from the Russian Federation and Central Asia are also included. The report only focuses on debt markets, and does not cover other forms of financing for green investments (e.g. project finance, private equity or venture capital). The analysis is based on information made publically available by the IFIs and local financial institutions (FIs), discussions with IFI stakeholders and relevant third party studies. The draft report was also discussed at an expert meeting held on 5-6 June 2014 at the OECD Headquarters in Paris.

The report has been developed within the framework of the project on "Greening Economies in the Eastern Neighbourhood" (EaP GREEN) funded by the European Commission and implemented by the OECD in partnership with the UNEP, UNIDO and UNECE.

The report was drafted by Matthew Savage (Oxford Consulting Partners) under the guidance of and with inputs by Nelly Petkova (Project Manager, OECD Environment Directorate). The report was reviewed by Brendan Gillespie and Angela Bularga (OECD Environment Directorate). Special thanks go to Angela Bularga for her overall help with the project and to Ivan Gerginov (Econoler SA) and Rafal Stanek (SST-Consult) for their substantive comments on earlier drafts of the report. Irina Massovets provided valuable administrative support and Reka Mazur and Lupita Johansson assisted with the processing of the publication. The authors would also like to thank Janine Trevis and Meral Gedik (OECD PAC) for editorial assistance. All these contributions are gratefully acknowledged.

Table of contents

Boxes

Tables

Figures

Abbreviations and Acronyms

ADB	Asian Development Bank
BAT	Best available technique
CA	Central Asia
CEE	Central and Eastern Europe
CIS	Commonwealth of Independent States
CLIM	Climate Laws Institutions and Measures Index (EBRD)
CSR	Corporate social responsibility
CTF	Clean Technology Fund
EBRD	European Bank for Reconstruction and Development
EE	Energy efficiency
EECCA	Eastern Europe, Caucus and Central Asia
EIB	European Investment Bank
ESCO	Energy service company
ESMS	Environmental and social management system
EU EaP	European Union Eastern Partnership
FDI	Foreign direct investment
FI	Financial Institution
GCPF	Global Climate Partnership Fund
GDP	Gross domestic product
GHG	Greenhouse gas
GNI	Gross national income
GWh	Gigawatt hour
IBRD	International Bank for Reconstruction and Development
IEA	International Energy Agency
IFC	International Finance Corporation
IFI	International Finance Institution
IMF	International Monetary Fund
ISE	Index of sustainable energy

KFW	German Development Bank
LEME	List of eligible materials and equipment
LESI	List of equipment supplies and installers
MFI	Micro-finance institution
mln	Million
MSME	Micro, small and medium sized enterprise
MWh	Megawatt hour
NEFCO	Nordic Environment Finance Corporation
NPL	Non-performing loan
OECD	Organisation for Economic Co-operation and Development
OeDB	Austrian Development Bank
PB	Participating bank
PPCR	Pilot Programme for Climate Resilience
R&D	Research and development
RE	Renewable energy
SE	Sustainable energy
SEFF	Sustainable Energy Finance Facility
SME	Small and medium sized enterprise
SOB	State owned bank
TA	Technical assistance
TC	Technical cooperation
tCO_2e	Tons of carbon dioxide equivalent
UAH	Ukrainian hryvna
Ukreximbank	State Export-Import Bank of Ukraine
USD	US dollar
WB	World Bank

Executive Summary

The financial and capital markets in the European Union's Eastern Partnership (EaP) countries remain under-developed, with commercial banks having a dominant position. While foreign funding remains commonplace in the region, and foreign currency lending continues, there is a process of consolidation and a move towards more sustainable lending models financed by domestic savings. However, local banks are likely to face a range of new challenges, including new and stricter regulations, higher funding and risk costs, especially for longer-term investments with unfamiliar risk profile, and changing customer behaviour. This, combined with a period of slow global growth, a long period of deleveraging, and higher levels of market volatility is likely to make it more difficult for banks to provide more lending to customers and deliver shareholder returns above the costs of capital.

Nonetheless, a more competitive domestic banking sector, with smaller numbers of better capitalised and more professional financial institutions will drive the need to innovate in terms of product offering. Access to surplus capital has the potential to make environmental lending a more attractive opportunity, as banks pursue strategies of market segmentation and seek to differentiate themselves from rivals. Environmental credit lines extended by International Finance Institutions (IFIs) and disbursed through local commercial banks provide an example in this direction.

Main findings of the report

Environmental credit lines provided by IFIs and on-lent by local banks aim to promote green investments in the EaP countries. Generally, IFIs are committed to not distorting commercial lending markets unless there is a clear market failure and associated development benefit. In addition to supporting immediate investment priorities, IFIs have established such credit lines with the aim of supporting local banks to create sustainable energy lending products as part of their standard offering. Such credit lines also aim to demonstrate the commercial viability of green financing as an attractive business model, thus laying the basis for a self-sustaining market for financing sustainable energy projects in these countries.

The main findings that have emerged from the analysis include:

- At least 8 IFIs (the European Bank for Reconstruction and Development (EBRD), the International Finance Corporation, the European Investment Bank, the World Bank, the Asian Development Bank, KfW, the Austrian Development Bank, and the Nordic Environment Finance Corporation) have extended environmental credit lines to the EaP countries, the Russian Federation and Central Asia. These credit lines have been mostly focused on energy efficiency (industrial, small and medium-sized enterprises (SMEs), residential and housing) and small-scale renewable energy. In addition, there are several multilateral facilities and donor financed platforms that have also issued environmental credit lines to local financial institutions (FIs) in the region (e.g. Green for Growth Fund, Global Climate Partnership Fund, E5P Fund).

- In total, approximately EUR 800 million has been committed by the IFIs in the EaP countries to date, with a further EUR 500 million in the Russian Federation and Central Asia. The two countries that have benefitted most are the Russian Federation and Ukraine, each with just under EUR 500 million in credit lines since 2006. There is approximately another EUR 300 million of additional environmental credit lines currently under various stages of negotiation. EBRD (through its Sustainable Energy Financing Facilities) is the most significant financier in the region. By end 2013, it had EUR 346 million of credit agreements with local banks in the EaP countries.
- In total, about 70 banks in the region have received support, of which approximately half are in the EaP countries. Several local FIs have agreed more than one credit line often with multiple IFIs. The State Export-Import Bank of Ukraine (Ukreximbank) has the largest portfolio of IFI-supported credit lines in the region.
- The cost of IFI funds is often not the lowest available to commercial banks. However, interest rates offered on IFI environmental credit lines may be more concessional than for other products (such as SME credit lines), making them more attractive for local financing institutions. Lower rates may be achieved through the blending of donor grant finance, or by IFI board approval based on the expected demonstration effect. Tenor, however, is often longer than that available elsewhere and this is a key factor for many local FIs to engage.
- Most credit lines are accompanied by some form of (donor-financed) technical assistance for the local financial institution. A number of local banks have received capacity building support alongside the credit line.

Key messages

Some of the key messages that emerge from the analysis include:

- Despite a growing number of local FIs involved, environmental lending in the EaP countries remains at an early stage of development. The supply of IFI finance is not sufficient to change the market dynamics by itself. A supportive regulatory and policy environment was identified as critically important to ensure the development of demand for green investments. Supporting local FIs to improve their capacity as well as raising awareness and knowledge of the benefits from investing in green projects among potential borrowers is also critical.
- IFIs need to demonstrate the commercial sustainability of green lending by keeping concessionality to a minimum where there is already a positive financial investment case. Technical assistance and incentives are useful for overcoming behavioural barriers, but should not be used to subsidise economically non-viable projects. IFIs should help FIs to migrate to a sustainable long-term lending model, and the structure of credit lines needs to fit the resource and institutional constraints of the FIs. Going forward, IFIs may have to broaden their role towards de-risking the flow of third party public and private finance, rather than to meeting their own lending targets.

- While most IFIs set environmental performance indicators for their credit lines, commercial and performance information associated with IFI portfolios is generally not made publically available. This makes it more difficult to judge the sustainability and leveraging effect of IFI funds disbursed through environmental credit lines. It should be noted that within the G20 framework, IFIs have been required to report on private sector leveraging and support for lending for market development.
- Additional country-level analysis is needed in order to produce country-specific recommendations with regard to better promoting the access to private finance for green investments in the EaP countries. Working jointly with local commercial banks, IFIs and relevant government agencies can help strengthen the analysis. It can help develop a shared understanding among major stakeholders of the key measures that need to be taken in order to facilitate access of private sector actors to long-term funding for low-carbon investments.

Chapter 1.

Government role in creating demand for green investments

This chapter discusses some of the major factors that shape the demand for and supply of long-term bank financing for green investments and sets the scene for the analysis of environmental lending in the EU's Eastern Partnership countries. The existence of a strong banking sector is an essential prerequisite for investing in low-carbon projects. However, governments have a crucial role to play in putting in place an appropriate policy and regulatory framework that can create a green investment climate and encourage market participants to undertake and finance green investments.

This chapter also outlines possible further work as well as describes the research approach and methodology that are envisaged to be applied in potential future country level analysis.

While the focus of this report is on the supply of long-term green lending, offered through International Finance Institution (IFI)-supported credit lines and disbursed through local banks, understanding the factors that shape the demand for such financing – actions that governments undertake to define objectives, set targets, elaborate policy instruments and monitor responses of households and businesses – are equally important.

Experience to date has shown that when taking environmental credit, end borrowers in the EU's Eastern Partnership (EaP) countries are more driven by economic than environmental concerns. Green investments are usually seen as relatively risky and non-profitable, as many of the technologies are still at a nascent stage and can be higher cost than prevailing alternatives. The absence of good information about the payback periods of particular investments and the relatively low price of energy in many of the countries constitute a major barrier to increased demand for green investments. In addition, local capital markets and financial institutions are still not adequately developed and lack the capacity to design sophisticated instruments and mobilise long-term finance. Critical actors on the supply side, such as leasing firms, equity and investment funds that can provide equity to leverage debt from the banks are only slowly emerging. In such a situation, IFIs remain the most important source of long-term wholesale funding in the region.

Demand for and supply of long-term green lending

The existence of a strong banking sector is an essential prerequisite for investing in low-carbon projects. Governments have a crucial role to play in putting in place an appropriate legal and policy framework that can allow capital markets to function properly. At the same time, governments can use a wide array of policy tools to create a green investment climate and encourage market participants to undertake and finance green projects.

These tools range from policies and legislation that can help advance environmental goals (e.g. defining key energy targets and energy conservation measures, specific greenhouse gas (GHG) emission reduction objectives, designing macroeconomic and trade policies that influence prices, developing regulations that remove perverse incentives that encourage excessive use of energy) to public programmes that support the implementation of policy objectives (e.g. public sector procurement, provision of information, product labelling), and regulatory and enforcement tools (e.g. permitting, environmental quality standards).

While the main thrust of these policies is to encourage companies and households to undertake appropriate investments, market participants will respond favourably if they have the flexibility to do so at the lowest possible cost. Market instruments that reduce barriers and costs for investors to access appropriate technologies (e.g. minimal tariffs or import duties) or provide investment incentives (e.g. tax credits) encourage more cost-effective funding of environmental investments.

A large number of financial instruments can also be applied in support of the scaling up of green investments. These include, among others, grants, government loans and guarantees, bonds, feed-in tariffs, credit lines, equity funds, venture capital. Only a few of these instruments however are actually available in the EaP countries.

In order to correct some of the market failures and to promote green investments in the region, a number of IFIs have established credit lines earmarked for environmental purposes. In addition to supporting immediate investment priorities, IFIs have provided such credit lines with the aim of helping develop the capacity of local banks to internalise sustainable environmental, and particularly energy, lending into their standard product portfolio. IFIs have also aimed to demonstrate the commercial viability of green finance as an attractive business opportunity, thus laying the foundations for a self-sustaining market in these countries. Over time, the aim is to move from a model based on concessional finance and donor-funded technical assistance towards a fully commercial approach. However, this will only happen if local banks see sufficient market opportunity (compared to competing segments) and if they are prepared to make the necessary investments in products, staff and capacity. This, in turn, requires sufficient demand from borrowers and a supportive public policy framework.

In order to estimate the overall demand for green investments, EaP governments need to establish clear policy objectives and SMART (simple, measurable, achievable, realistic and time-bound) targets for the specific sector (e.g. energy). On this basis, they can determine the costs, financing needs and funding gaps.

However, countries in the region do not generally have such strategies. As a result, it is not obvious to what extent IFI-supported environmental credit lines are contributing to the achievement of national (energy) priorities and targets. Some countries have developed or are in the process of developing Green Growth Strategies which may contain sections on energy, water security or energy conservation but these do not generally have detailed estimates of the financing needed and the possible ways to close the financing gap. This is a policy area which deserves special attention and is one where donor and IFIs support may have a critical impact.

Figure 1.1. **Elements of green investment climate**

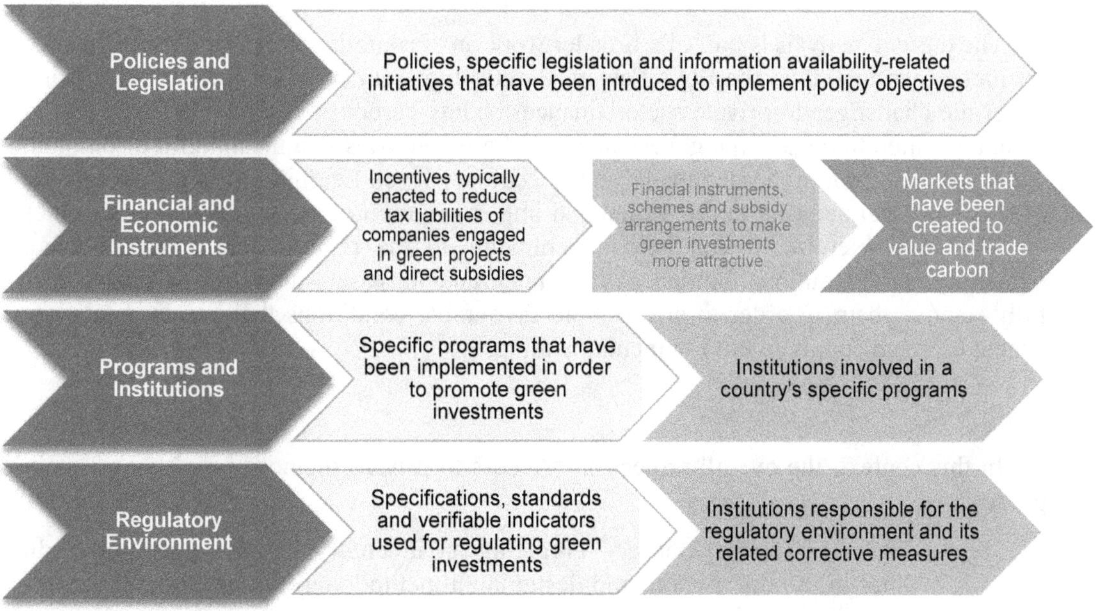

Source: World Bank (2012).

One particular issue that needs at least a brief discussion in this context is the definition of "green investments". A summary of the OECD's thinking in this regard is presented in Box 1.1 below.

For the purposes of this report, we adopt the below broad definition and use all the below terms interchangeably.

Box 1.1. **Definition of "green" investments**

There is no consensus on what exactly constitutes green investment. There are actually a number of definitions that circulate in the market place. Definitions of "green" can be explicit or implicit. Some are very broad and generic, others are more technical and specific. Some are investment-driven, others come out of ecological or ethical discussions. "Green investments" are often variously referred to as "clean", "sustainable", "climate change", "low-carbon", "environmental" or "environmentally-related" investments.

Investors' attention to climate change, resource efficiency and green issues, in general, has been rising in recent years and investor initiatives in this respect are growing in support. Sometimes, two or more concepts are applied at the same time by investors. The preferences for the various concepts vary across countries and investors, and historical, cultural and regulatory reasons play their role.

Generally, however people converge around the idea that investments in sustainable energy, energy efficiency, renewable sources of energy, recycling and waste management, wastewater treatment or clean transport constitute green types of investment.

Source: Adopted from Inderst, G et al. (2012).

Plans for future work

The current analysis is part of a broader work on "Promoting access to private finance for green investments in the EU's Eastern Partnership countries". In order to understand better the challenges to private sector finance for low-carbon investment projects and to be in a position to engage the governments of these countries in a meaningful discussion, there is a need for more in-depth analysis at a country level. Learning from the experience of IFIs and local banks with the design and implementation of environmental credit lines is a valuable exercise. It can help governments in the region identify actual legal, regulatory and institutional bottlenecks and undertake necessary measures to minimise or fully remove them in order to create more favourable conditions that can lead to more demand for and supply of environmental lending.

Main phases of the project

In this context, the overall project on "Access to private finance" consists of 3 main phases:

- Phase 1: Scoping phase – Preparing an inventory of environmental credit lines in the EaP region, and designing a methodology for an in-depth review of such credit lines (current work);
- Phase 2: Country level work – Conducting in-depth reviews of selected credit lines in 2-3 EaP countries;
- Phase 3: Developing conclusions and recommendations – Summarising the lessons learnt from the implementation of the reviewed credit lines and

organising a region-wide policy dialogue on access to private finance for green investments.

Figure 1.2 below shows the main elements of each of the three phases.

Figure 1.2. **Main phases of the project**

Phase 1: Scoping: inventory of credit lines, data and development of methodology			
Inventory of existing credit lines	Checking availability of performance information and other conditions for the in-depth analysis	Development of the methodology for in-depth analysis	Dialogue with IFIs and local banks, including an expert meeting

Phase 2: In-depth country-level analysis of specific credit lines relevant for green growth				
Selection of countries and credit lines for analysis	Data gathering	Interviews with local stakeholders	Drafting case studies	Discussing results of analysis with stakeholders

Phase 3: Development of recommendations and policy dialogue				
Consolidation of case studies	Summarising key lessons learned from the implementation of IFI credit lines	Identification of conditions for increasing demand for green investments	Identification of conditions for making green credits a viable local business model	Organisation of an international conference

Possible criteria for selection of country level case studies

The implementation of Phase 2 of the project largely depends on the willingness of the local banks in the EaP region to participate in this study. To have a relevant discussion at a country level, there needs to be a concerted effort; therefore, support by the respective government and relevant IFIs will be also very important. Such a joint effort will allow us to share the results of the project more broadly, both across the EaP countries as well as across IFIs that may be interested in the results of the analysis.

In order to identify potential case studies for more detailed analysis, we suggest a few criteria to be applied in the selection process. These criteria are not meant to be exhaustive or to provide ultimate authority. They are rather intended to help launch and focus the discussion. These criteria are briefly described below.

- *Sector coverage:* The selection of case studies should seek to maximise the number of different end borrower segments that can be examined. These should include corporate, small and medium sized enterprises (SME), residential and renewable energy. Some banks cover more than one sector through a single IFI credit line.
- *Market profile and opportunity to scale:* The case studies should reflect different market characteristics. At least one case study could be taken from a larger industrial economy (e.g., Ukraine, Belarus) with a higher number of local financial institutions and greater potential market volumes, together with at least one credit line in a smaller less industrial economy (e.g. Caucasus, Moldova) with more limited market size and a potentially less competitive environment.
- *Policy environment:* The case studies should cover at least one economy that has developed supportive environmental policies, together with one that remains in the early stage of introducing sustainable energy, environmental and greenhouse gas emission reduction support mechanisms. In both cases, there should be some activity

by IFIs to engage with the government on policy and regulatory reform. This will allow an analysis of the role played by the policy environment in supporting environmental lending, and the challenges faced by IFIs in engaging on these topics.

- *Sustainability:* The case studies should include at least one local financial institution that has gone on to resource on its own and support an environmental loan product following full disbursement of the IFI credit line (or at least negotiated a follow on tranche from the same or another IFI) together with at least one financial institution that has decided not to pursue the market segment on the basis of experience. This will allow for an examination of the motivations and barriers to building sustainable lending products.
- *Support by multiple FIs:* The case studies should seek to include at least one local financial institution that has received funding and technical assistance from more than one IFI or donor. This will allow for a discussion on the relative merits of donor approaches, and help identify the key elements of support that IFIs can deliver to support supply side development.
- *Willingness to participate:* There should be agreement both with the IFI and the local financial institution to participate. Without the consent of both of them, it is unlikely that the project team will receive sufficient access to staff and data to complete the Phase 2 review. Government support for the project will also be crucial.

Research approach

In order to conduct the country case studies and make them more focused, we propose a research method which is briefly described below.

The aim of this research will be to test the hypothesis of the key success drivers, set out in Chapter 6 (namely, FI engagement, financial product delivery, market environment in which environmental lending products are delivered), analyse potential barriers and identify areas where policy makers, IFIs and donors could provide further critical support. The research approach consists of 3 main components which include collection of data and information using: factual data table, semi-structured questionnaire and market review.

Factual data table

The data table provides a template for the collection of quantitative and factual data from the participating local financial institution and the partner IFI (see Annex A.1). This table will be used to collect relevant information prior to engaging with the stakeholders on a face-to-face basis in the country. It incorporates the elements of data analysis set out in the regional review of current credit lines. The aim is to establish the parameters and performance of the credit line.

Semi-structured questionnaire

The semi-structured questionnaire is presented in Annex A.2. This questionnaire serves as an interview guide for engaging with the range of stakeholders as identified in Figure 1.3. The questionnaire is organised around 4 thematic sections: (i) IFI engagement with IFs; (ii) product design and delivery; (iii) monitoring, reporting and verification; and, (iv) sustainability of products offered through the credit line. Each section has a number of sub-sections addressing particular aspects of credit line design and implementation. As indicated in the Annex A, each question may be relevant to more than one stakeholder.

Market review

For each credit line, we will undertake a desk review of the current state of policy and market development. This will allow for an in-depth assessment of the context in which the credit line has been designed. The market review approach is briefly described in Annex B.

Stakeholders

Stakeholders that can potentially be engaged in the research process include relevant IFIs, staff of local financial institutions, end borrowers, policy makers and other influencers. These are set out in Figure 1.3 below.

Figure 1.3. **Key stakeholders for consultations**

IFI staff and consultants

- IFI Financial Markets Product staff
- IFI Technical assistance and product advisory staff
- IFI Consultants (capacity building, technical and monitoring, reporting and verification)

FI staff

- Senior management (executive team)
- Product managers (e.g. energy efficiency, innovative products)
- Loan officers (central Headquarters and regional)
- Marketing officer (product promotion and communication)
- Shareholders and board members (strategic direction, accountability)

End borrowers

- Senior management (decision makers)
- Financial department (profitability)
- Technical/engineering (productivity, environmental)

Policy makers

- Ministry of Finance (subsidies, fiscal position)
- Ministry of Enivronment (legislation, regulation)
- Ministry of Energy (energy pricing, strategy)
- Other relevant government agencies

Influencers

- Donors
- NGOs and campaign organisations
- Academics and research community

References

Cochran, I. et al. (2014), "Public Financial Institutions and the Low-Carbon Transition: Five Case Studies on Low-Carbon Infrastructure and Project Investment", *OECD Environment Working Papers*, No. 72, OECD Publishing, Paris, http://dx.doi.org/10.1787/5jxt3rhpgn9t-en

Corfee-Morlot, J. et al. (2012), "Towards a Green Investment Policy Framework: The Case of Low-Carbon, Climate-Resilient Infrastructure", *OECD Environment Working Papers,* No. 48, OECD Publishing, Paris, http://dx.doi.org/10.1787/5k8zth7s6s6d-en

Inderst, G., Kaminker, Ch. and Stewart, F. (2012), "Defining and Measuring Green Investments: Implications for Institutional Investors' Asset Allocations", *OECD Working Papers on Finance, Insurance and Private Pensions*, No. 24, OECD Publishing, Paris, http://dx.doi.org/10.1787/5k9312twnn44-en

OECD (2015), *Policy Guidance for Investment in Clean Energy Infrastructure - Expanding Access to Clean Energy for Green Growth and Development*, OECD Publishing, Paris, http://dx.doi.org/10.1787/9789264212664-en

OECD (2012), *Greening Public Budgets in Eastern Europe, Caucasus and Central Asia*, OECD Publishing, Paris, http://dx.doi.org/10.1787/9789264118331-en

UNEP FI (2007), *Green Financial Products and Services: Current Trends and Future Opportunities in North America - A Report of the North American Task Force of the UNEP FI*, Prepared by ICF Consulting Canada, Inc., UNEP FI, Geneva, www.unepfi.org/fileadmin/documents/greenprods_01.pdf

World Bank (2012), *Green Infrastructure Finance - Framework Report*, World Bank Study, World Bank, Washington DC, www10.iadb.org/intal/intalcdi/pe/2012/10331.pdf

World Economic Forum (2013), *The Green Growth Action Alliance: Progress Report from the First Year of Catalysing Private Investmen*t, World Economic Forum, www3.weforum.org/docs/IP/2013/ENVI/GreenGrowthActionAlliance_2013.pdf

Chapter 2.

Macroeconomic context and the banking sector in the EaP countries

This chapter looks at the major macroeconomic and environmental factors that shape the context in which green lending in the EU's Eastern Partnership countries, but also in the Russian Federation and Central Asia, takes place. The chapter also briefly discusses the status of the banking sector in the region as a backdrop against which environmentally-related credit lines, supported by International Finance Institutions, will be further analysed.

Macroeconomic performance

In the EU's Eastern Partnership (EaP) countries, the economic, social and environmental changes of the transition period have taken place in a dynamic national and international context, most recently impacted by the 2008 world financial and economic crisis and the political crisis in Ukraine.

Prior to 2008, these countries generally enjoyed stable economic growth. According to the World Bank classification of the world's economies based on estimates of gross national income (GNI) per capita, in 2015, four EaP countries – Armenia, Georgia, Moldova and Ukraine – were classified as lower middle-income countries (at USD 1 046 – to 4 125 per capita) and two countries – Azerbaijan and Belarus – as upper middle-income countries (at USD 4 126 to 12 745 per capita).

The EaP countries were particularly badly hit by the 2008 crisis, with Armenia and Azerbaijan experiencing the most severe economic downturn. As a result of the crisis, economic activity shrunk rapidly and bank credit also began to contract significantly. The international response to the crisis in the region included large-scale balance-of-payments support for some of the countries. The International Monetary Fund (IMF) agreed such programmes for a number of countries in the region. Most recently, in May 2014, IMF granted a USD 17 billion aid package to Ukraine and in March 2015 IMF approved another loan of USD 17.5 billion to help the country stabilise the economy and the financial sector and overcome the current political crisis.

Growth in the region has been volatile and has relied heavily on energy resources (Azerbaijan), other commodities (Ukraine), and remittances (Armenia, Moldova). After the peak of the crisis, growth resumed in 2010 but since 2012 it has generally slowed again in most of the countries in the region. Moldova is a notable exception. After a negative economic growth in 2012, the country's economy grew at a rate of about 9% in 2013.

2014 data show that generally growth in the EaP countries worsened, amid tensions in Ukraine. Only Belarus and Georgia saw their economies grow in 2014 compared to the previous year. According to EBRD, in 2014, the crisis in Ukraine, the substantial slowdown in the Russian Federation and the rapidly increasing geopolitical risks in the region, as well as the likelihood of negative cross-border economic and financial spill-overs constrained economic activity in the region even further.

As a result of the earlier financial crisis and slowing economic activity, the fiscal position of the EaP countries has weakened by the generally low level of government tax revenue as a percentage of GDP. The region's fiscal deficits have come down from the crisis highs but are projected to deteriorate in 2014 and 2015.

Figure 2.1. **GDP growth (annual %), EaP countries, Kazakhstan and Russia, 2009 - 2014**

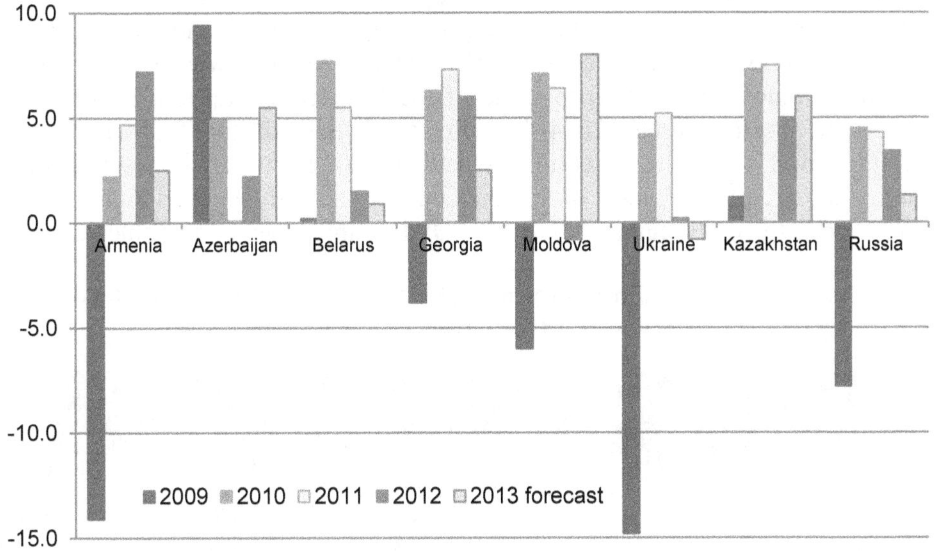

Source: World Bank, World Development Indicators database. http://data.worldbank.org/indicator/NE.GDI.TOTL.ZS/countries, accessed 28 October 2015.

Compared to pre-crisis levels, inflation has been largely curbed, but it also remains volatile. Inflation is high in Belarus (more than 18%). In Ukraine, inflation has been on the rise and as of June 2015, it topped 60% due, mostly, to utility price hikes. Kazakhstan and the Russian Federation have seen inflation rise as well.

Table 2.1. **Major macroeconomic indicators, EaP countries, Kazakhstan and Russia, 2014**

Country	Population, *million inhabitants*	GDP, *billion*	GDP per capita	FDI inflows, *million*	GDP growth	Inflation, consumer prices	General government tax revenue	General government expenditure	Gash surplus / deficit	General government debt	Gross capital formation	Domestic credit provided by financial sector
		USD			*annual %*		*% of GDP**					
ARM	3.0	10.9	3620	404	3.4	3.0	18.7	22.8	-1.4		20	54.9
AZE	9.5	75.2	7884	4431	2.0	1.4	13	22.5	6.1		26	33.8
BLR	9.5	76.1	8040	1833	1.6	18.1	15.1	28.5	0.1	25.2	33	42.8
GEO	4.5	16.5	3670	1274	4.8	3.1	24.1	25.4	-0.5	32.5	30	48.5
MDL	3.6	7.9	2234	353	4.6	5.1	18.6	33.3	-2.0	24.3	26	39.0
UKR	45.5	131.8	3083	847	-6.8	12.2	18.3	41.1	-4.1	33.7	14	110.0
KAZ	17.3	212.2	12276	9739**	4.3	6.7					24**	37.6
RUS	143.8	1860.6	12736	22857	0.6	7.8	15.1	26.4	2.7	9.4	23**	52.4

Note: * Indicates data for 2012; ** Indicates data for 2013.

Source: World Bank, World Development Indicators database. http://data.worldbank.org/indicator/NE.GDI.TOTL.ZS/countries, accessed 28 October 2015.

World Bank data show that domestic investments in Azerbaijan, Georgia and Moldova (measured as gross capital formation as a share of GDP) increased over the period 2011 – 2014. At the same time, Armenia, Belarus and Ukraine saw a decrease in domestic investment levels. Over the same period and both in absolute terms and as a share of GDP, foreign direct investment (FDI) increased, somewhat slightly, only in Georgia and Moldova. Compared to some of the Central and Eastern Europe (CEE) economies, in absolute terms, 2014 FDI flows in most of the EaP countries are significantly lower (with the exception of Azerbaijan). However, between 2011 and 2014 and as a share of GDP, most of the EaP countries actually enjoyed higher levels of FDI compared to the CEE region. Aggregate FDI data are presented in Table 2.2 below.

Table 2.2. **Foreign direct investment, EaP countries, Kazakhstan, Russia and selected EU countries, 2011 and 2014**

Country	FDI, net inflows (% of GDP)		FDI, net inflows (Balance of payments, current USD million)	
	2011	*2014*	*2011*	*2014*
ARM	6.4	3.7	653	404
AZE	6.8	5.9	4 485	4 431
BLR	6.7	2.4	4 402	1 833
GEO	7.5	7.7	1 084	1 274
MDL	4.3	4.4	301	353
UKR	4.7	2.5	7 207	847
KAZ	7.3	4.2*	13 760	9 739*
RUS	2.9	1.2	55 084	22 857
BGR	3.8	3.6	2 124	2 028
CZE	1.8	2.4	4 189	4 871
ROU	1.4	1.7	2 557	3 402
SVK	3.8	0.9	3 658	896

Note: (*) Indicates data for 2013.

Source: World Bank, World Development Indicators database. http://data.worldbank.org/indicator/NE.GDI.TOTL.ZS/countries, accessed 28 October 2015.

Despite the increase in GDP growth and investment levels, the countries in the region are still facing significant environmental challenges, partly inherited from the Soviet Union and partly newly acquired as a result of modern consumption patterns. Waste management systems (where they exist at all) fail to correspond to the expanding variety of materials produced by the consumer society, tap water is not potable in many places, and air pollution from transport and burning coal plagues numerous cities. Extraction of natural resources proceeds at a fast pace and fossil fuel subsidies still persist in a number of countries. As reported by the International Energy Agency (IEA), Azerbaijan, Ukraine, Kazakhstan and the Russian Federation are among the top 25 non-OECD countries with the highest levels of fossil fuel consumer subsidies. For example, in 2012, these subsidies ranged from USD 2 billion in Azerbaijan (equivalent to 3.3% of GDP) to USD 11 billion in Ukraine (6.1% of GDP). The energy and carbon intensity of many of these economies remains far above the OECD and EU average (see Figure 2.2).

Dealing with environmental problems in the region will require significant resources, both public and private. A 2012 survey of medium-term budgetary practices in these countries, conducted by OECD, showed that on average, in 2009, countries in the region spent less than 0.5% of GDP on public environmental expenditure. On a per capita basis, this expenditure was also low and in 2009 ranged from less than USD 1 per capita in Georgia to about USD 70 per capita in Belarus (OECD, 2012). For comparison, public environmentally-related expenditure in OECD countries is on average about 1%. The magnitude of environmental challenges in the region shows that the public sector alone cannot solve these problems. Private sector resources, including through commercial banking sector lending, are needed to support government efforts.

Figure 2.2. **Carbon and energy intensities, EaP countries and selected OECD and emerging economies, 2012**

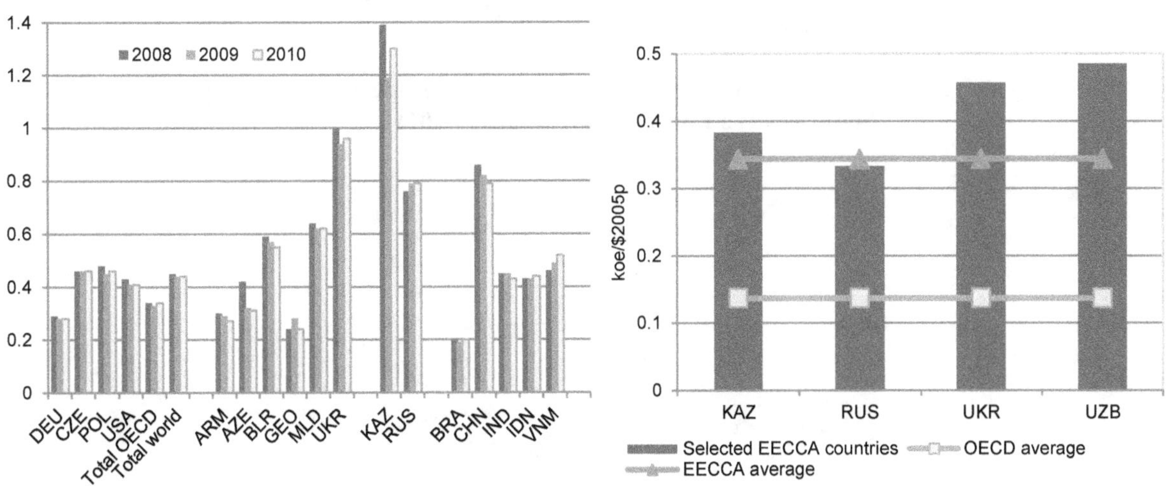

Source: IEA (2014).

Source: Enerdata, http://www.enerdata.net/enerdatauk/knowledge/subscriptions/database/.

Banking sector development

There was a rapid expansion of the commercial banking sector in the EaP countries over the period 2000-2007. In 2000, banking penetration in Eastern Europe (as measured by the ratio of lending volumes to GDP) was lower than that in other emerging markets, for example in China or Latin America. Analysis by McKinsey (2012) indicates that Eastern European banking revenues from loans and deposits (excluding the Russian Federation) grew by more than 14% a year on average between 2000 and 2007. This was more than three times the global average growth rate of 4.1% and higher than both India and China over the same timeframe. During this time, Western European banks took positions in many of these markets.

Increased access to lower cost funds created a number of economic imbalances, including a rapid expansion of services and the non-traded sector, the appearance of asset price bubbles, and a growth in unhedged foreign currency lending. Banks set up expensive branch networks on the basis of small transaction volumes (less than one tenth of their European equivalents) and lower disposable household income (approximately one fifth). As a result, although growth was rapid, value creation (defined as return on equity less cost of capital) was low. Risk and governance procedures were also weak.

These imbalances became apparent during the financial crisis in 2008. International capital became more scarce and expensive, although western banks received support under the 'Vienna Initiative'[1] to remain committed to the region. Ukraine suffered a systemic banking crisis among its domestically-owned banks. The official levels of non-performing loans (NPLs) increased across the region. However, many banks in the region have chosen to roll over problematic lending, waiting for a recovery in loan quality and collateral value.

Officially, non-performing loans for banks in the countries of Eastern Europe, Caucasus and Central Asia (EECCA) (also referred to as Commonwealth of Independent States (CIS) remain lower than for those in other regions (see Figure 2.3). Nonetheless, there remains a significant debt overhang (EIB, 2013a).

Figure 2.3. **Ratio of non-performing loans in Western Europe, Central Europe, South Eastern Europe and CIS, 2000 - 2011**

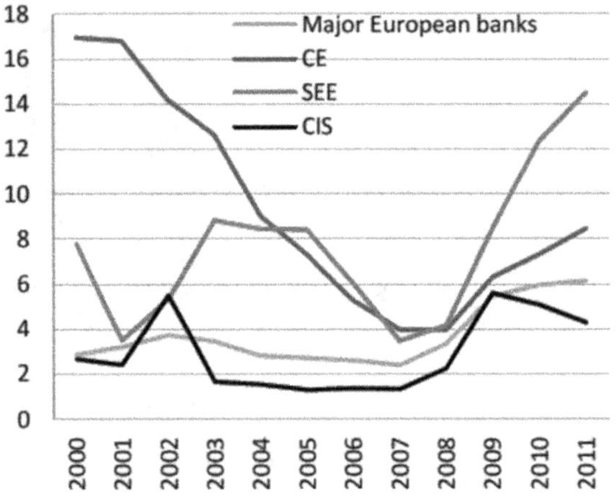

Source: EIB (2013a).

At the present time, while foreign funding remains commonplace in the region, and foreign currency lending continues, there is a process of consolidation and a move towards more sustainable lending models financed by domestic savings. The number of banks remains high and a process of consolidation is likely to continue. Most of the banks have been privatised and very few state-owned banks have remained. Table 2.3 sets out the number of financial institutions in the region as of 2012, together with key banking sector data.

Table 2.3. **Number of banks in the EaP countries, 2012 (excluding Belarus)**

	ARM	AZE	GEO	MDL	UKR
Banks	22	43	19	14	184*
- Of which stated owned banks (SOB)		1	0	1	2
- Assets of SOBs to total	0	37%	0	9%	11%
- 5 Bank Concentration Ratio	48.6%	58.3%	92.4%	70.3%	31.6%
- Total net loans (EUR mln)	3 101	10 270	3 722	2 129	68 522
- Non-performing loans (NPL)	3.7%	6.5%	3.7%	14.5%	3.5%
Microfinance institutions (MFIs)	12	30	60	60	1
Leasing companies	3	8	25	25	21
Private equity/Venture capital firms	2	2	5	5	13

Note: (*) Since the early 2014, more than 50 banks have been withdrawn from the market in Ukraine, 13 of them were declared insolvent since the beginning of 2015.

Source: EIB (2013b).

On the whole, financial markets in the EECCA countries continue to be rated relatively poorly by international ranking processes in relation to their international peers. For example, the World Economic Forum Global Competitiveness Report (2013) provides rankings for the countries in the region (excluding Belarus) for Financial Market Development.[2] Not a single EECCA country makes the top 50% of those reviewed.[3]

Table 2.4. **World Economic Forum: Financial market development in selected EECCA countries, 2012**

Country	Points score (7 max)	Rank (out of 148 economies)
Georgia	3.9	75
Armenia	3.9	76
Azerbaijan	3.8	88
Kazakhstan	3.7	103
Moldova	3.6	105
Kyrgyz Republic	3.5	112
Ukraine	3.5	117
Russia	3.4	121

Source: World Economic Forum (2013).

Banks in the region are likely to face a range of new challenges, including new regulations, higher funding and risk costs, and changing customer behavior. This, combined with a period of slow global growth, a long period of deleveraging, and higher levels of market volatility is likely to make it more difficult for banks to deliver shareholder returns above the costs of capital.

As banks repair their balance sheets and address the poor quality of their existing loan portfolios, domestic demand may remain subdued. Unaddressed, non-performing loans may create a drag on credit growth and keep capital deployed in unproductive uses. Several taxation and regulatory barriers exist that would also require sector reform by government to support this process.

Nonetheless, a more competitive banking environment, with smaller numbers of better capitalised and more professional financial institutions will drive the need to innovate in terms of product offering. This has the potential to make environmental lending a more attractive opportunity, as banks pursue strategies of market segmentation, and seek to differentiate themselves from rivals. Environmentally-related credit lines extended by International Finance Institutions and disbursed by local commercial banks provide an example in this direction.

Endnotes

1. The European Bank Coordination "Vienna" Initiative is a framework for safeguarding the financial stability of emerging Europe. The Initiative was launched at the height of the first wave of the global financial crisis in January 2009. It brought together all the relevant public and private sector stakeholders of EU-based cross-border banks active in emerging Europe, which own much of the banking sectors in that region and also hold a significant part of government securities.

2. The Financial Market Development is a composite index measuring availability and affordability of financial services, capacity to raise equity on local markets, ease of access to loans, availability of venture capital, soundness of banks, regulation of securities exchange and legal rights.

3. The World Bank Doing Business report provides similar rankings.

References

EIB (2013a), *Banking in Central and Eastern Europe and Turkey. Challenges and Opportunities*, EIB, Luxembourg, http://vienna-initiative.com/wp-content/uploads/2013/02/Banking-in-Central-and-Eastern-Europe-and-Turkey-Challenges-and-Opportunities.pdf

EIB (2013b), *Private Sector Financing in the Eastern Partnership Countries and the Role of Risk-Bearing Instruments*. Synthesis Report, November 2013, EIB, Luxembourg, www.eib.org/attachments/efs/econ_synthesis_report_psf_and_the_role_of_rbi_en.pdf

EIB (2012), *Banking in the Eastern Neighbours and Central Asia, Challenges and Opportunities,* EIB, Luxembourg, www.eib.org/attachments/efs/economic_report_banking_enca_en.pdf

Enerdata World Energy Database, www.enerdata.net/enerdatauk/knowledge/subscriptions/database/

Inderst, G., Kaminker, Ch., Stewart, F. (2012), "Defining and Measuring Green Investments: Implications for Institutional Investors' Asset Allocations", *OECD Working Papers on Finance, Insurance And Private Pensions*, No. 24, OECD Publishing, Paris, http://dx.doi.org/10.1787/5k9312twnn44-en

IEA (2014), *CO_2 emissions from Fuel Combustion 2014*, IEA, Paris, http://dx.doi.org/10.1787/co2_fuel-2014-en

McKinsey (2012), *What's Ahead for Banking in Eastern Europe*, available from www.mckinsey.com/insights/financial_services/whats_ahead_for_banking_in_eastern_europe

OECD (2012), *Greening Public Budgets in Eastern Europe, Caucasus and Central Asia*, OECD Publishing, Paris, http://dx.doi.org/10.1787/9789264118331-en

World Bank (2014), *Doing Business 2014. Understanding Regulations for Small and Medium-Size Enterprises,* World Bank, Washington DC, www.doingbusiness.org/~/media/GIAWB/Doing%20Business/Documents/Annual-reports/English/DB14-Full-Report.pdf

World Bank, *World Development Indicators Database,* http://wdi.worldbank.org/tables

World Economic Forum (2013), *The Global Competitiveness Report 2013 - 2014*, Full Data Edition, Klaus Schwab, World Economic Forum, www3.weforum.org/docs/WEF_GlobalCompetitivenessReport_2013-14.pdf

Chapter 3.

Environmental credit lines in the EaP countries

This chapter provides an overview of the main environmentally-oriented credit lines established with the support of the major International Finance Institutions (IFIs) and donors active in the EU's Eastern Partnership countries. The analysis is organised around three main groups of institutions, namely: multilateral development banks, donor development banks and multilateral finance instruments. The chapter provides a consolidated view of the portfolio (historic and current) for each IFI together with commentary on any accompanying technical assistance programme provided either directly to the local financial institutions, to their clients or to the wider policy environment.

Overview of environmental credit lines

Credit lines extended by International Finance Institutions (IFIs) and disbursed through local banks are the main source of long-term financing for green investments in the EU's Eastern Partnership (EaP) countries. Local banks on-lend to private sector clients (households, small and medium-sized enterprises (SMEs), industrial companies and project developers). Such credit lines facilitate access to longer-term finance and make it more feasible to borrow. This does not mean the funds are necessarily cheaper than ordinary loans, but the end user and the local bank can often benefit from consultancy services and training to develop feasible projects. This helps to reduce the risk to the local banks, making them more willing to lend, and also improves the overall effectiveness of the investment.

Most of the IFIs active in the region have opened environmental credit lines with local financing institutions (FIs). For the sake of the discussion in this analysis, IFIs were grouped into Multilateral Development Banks, Donor Development Banks and Multilateral Finance Instruments. The IFIs reviewed in this report include: the European Bank for Reconstruction and Development (EBRD), the International Finance Corporation (IFC), the European Investment Bank (EIB), the World Bank (IBRD), the Asian Development Bank (ADB), KfW (Germany), the Austrian Development Bank (OEDB), and the Nordic Environment Finance Corporation (NEFCO). The review is based on publically available information from the IFIs and local FIs, discussions with IFI stakeholders and relevant third party studies. The geographic scope is the EU's EaP countries, plus the Russian Federation and Central Asia, where relevant.

We estimate that IFIs have worked with and extended environmental credit lines to about 70 banks in the Eastern Europe, Caucasus and Central Asia (EECCA) region, of which approximately half are in the EaP countries. Several of these banks have agreed more than one credit line and some have credit lines with multiple IFIs. The State Export-Import Bank of Ukraine (Ukreximbank) manages the biggest number of IFI-supported credit lines in the region. In total, approximately EUR 800 million has been committed by the IFIs in the EaP countries to date, with a further EUR 500 million in the Russian Federation and Central Asia[1]. We are aware of approximately another EUR 300 million of additional environmental credit lines currently under various stages of negotiation. A number of banks have also received capacity building and technical assistance support alongside the credit line.

All countries in the region have access to such credit lines to a greater or lesser extent. However, the two countries that have benefitted most from such lines are the Russian Federation and Ukraine, each with just under EUR 500 million in credit lines since 2006.

Table 3.1 provides an overview of the main credit lines discussed in this chapter. More details follow further.

Table 3.1. **Overview of environmental credit lines in EaP countries, Russia and Central Asia**

Finance institution	Credit facility	Country where implemented	Key focus of credit line	Sectors supported	Facility value (end 2013, unless otherwise noted)
A: Multilateral development banks					
EBRD	Sustainable Energy Financing Facility	▪ 6 EaP ▪ Russia ▪ Central Asia (Kyrgyz Rep.+ Kazakhstan)	▪ Energy efficiency (EE) ▪ Small-scale Renewable energy (RE)	Residential, Micro, small and medium-sized enterprises (MSMEs), corporate, industrial loans for agribusiness, food processing, manufacturing, industry, construction, services	▪ EaP countries – EUR 422 mln ▪ Russia + Central Asia (CA) – EUR 183 mln
IFC	Russia Sustainable Energy Finance Program	▪ Russia – main focus ▪ Armenia ▪ Azerbaijan ▪ Belarus ▪ Ukraine ▪ Central Asia	▪ EE	SMEs (privately owned) and residential buildings	▪ Russia (July 2012) – USD 242 mln for direct EE projects ▪ EaP + Russia + CA – credit lines – USD 100 mln ▪ Ukraine – USD 20 mln
	Clean Technology Fund (CTF)	▪ Ukraine	▪ EE	Commercial, SME, residential	▪ Ukraine – USD 85 mln (projected for 2014)
EIB	No specific environmental-ly-related credit lines	▪ Armenia ▪ Azerbaijan ▪ Georgia ▪ Moldova ▪ Kazakhstan ▪ Russia ▪ Ukraine ▪ Tajikistan	Focused on small and medium-sized enterprises (SMEs) having some explicit or implicit environmental orientation (climate change mitigation and adaptation)		▪ Total for EaP + Russia + CA – EUR 2.3 bln (not specifically green loans)
World Bank (IBRD)	Limited number of credit lines provided through government agencies or state-owned banks	▪ Ukraine ▪ Russia	▪ EE	Industrial and commercial companies, municipalities and municipal sector enterprises and Energy service companies (ESCOs)	▪ Ukraine – USD 200 mln ▪ Russia – USD 300 mln (under negotiation)
ADB	Access to green finance projects	▪ Caucasus ▪ Central Asia	▪ EE	SMEs Microfinance credit for residential EE	▪ Tajikistan – USD 8.8 mln
NEFCO	Investment Fund	▪ Ukraine ▪ Belarus	▪ EE ▪ RE	Residential and industrial Solar, biomass	▪ Ukraine – EUR 3 mln ▪ Belarus – EUR 1.5 mln +EUR 3 mln (under negotiation)

Finance institution	Credit facility	Country where implemented	Key focus of credit line	Sectors supported	Facility value (end 2013, unless otherwise noted)
B: Donor development banks					
KfW		▪ Ukraine ▪ Armenia ▪ Georgia	▪ EE ▪ RE	SMEs Hydropower development (Georgia)	▪ Ukraine: – USD 30 mln ▪ Georgia – EUR 25 mln ▪ Armenia – EUR 24 mln
OEDB		▪ Russia ▪ Armenia ▪ Georgia	▪ Combined SME/ EE		▪ Russia – USD 25 mln ▪ Armenia – USD 15 mln ▪ Georgia – USD 15 mln
C: Multilateral finance instruments					
Green for Growth	Established by KfW, EIB, EC, EBRD	▪ All EaP eligible ▪ Until now credit lines in Armenia and Ukraine	▪ EE ▪ RE	Residential MSMEs Corporate SME, Industry	▪ Armenia – EUR – 16.4 mln ▪ Ukraine – EUR 10 mln
Global Climate Partner-ship Fund	Established by IFC, KfW, EIB	▪ Intensive economies globally, incl. e.g. Ukraine	▪ EE or small scale RE	SMEs Power generation facilities Modernisation of production facilities and larger corporations	▪ Ukraine – USD 30 mln
E5P Fund	Multi-donor fund managed by EBRD Provides grants to support IFI loans	▪ Eastern European countries, incl. - Ukraine - Armenia - Georgia - Moldova	▪ EE	District heating, EE projects	

Multilateral development banks

A number of multilateral development banks, active in the region, have opened environmental credit lines in the EaP countries. The most active among these banks is EBRD, but the European Investments Bank, the Asian Development Bank and the World Bank have also provided such credit lines. The International Finance Corporation and NEFCO are included in and analysed as part of this group of financiers as well.

European Bank for Reconstruction and Development

Since 2006, EBRD has been implementing Sustainable Energy Financing Facilities (SEFFs) throughout the EaP region, as well as in the Russian Federation and Central Asia. The EBRD extends credit lines to local financial institutions that seek to develop sustainable energy financing as a permanent field of business. Finance for sustainable energy projects is provided for two key areas: energy efficiency (EE) and small-scale renewable energy (RE). Energy efficiency lending may encompass residential, micro, small and medium-sized enterprises (M)SME) or larger corporate loans, depending on the local market profile. Local financial institutions on-lend the funds to their clients.

SEFF financing for businesses typically ranges from a few hundred thousand to a few million euros to support the purchase and installation of equipment, systems or processes. Across the EBRD region, SEFF financing has supported diverse projects in virtually all sectors, ranging from agribusiness, food processing, and manufacturing to industry, construction and services.

Residential loans cover a few thousand to a few hundred thousand euros, most often to support improvements on the building envelope. Various groups have benefited from

SEFF loans including individual owners, groups of home owners and multi-apartment associations.

Portfolio size and structure

Among the IFIs, EBRD has the largest energy efficiency finance portfolio in the EaP region, the Russian Federation and Central Asia. As of the end of 2013, EBRD had signed credit agreements with banks to the value of EUR 345 million in the EaP countries, within total facility commitments of EUR 422 million. A further EUR 183 million committed in the Russian Federation and Central Asia.

- *Armenia:* Branded as Energocredit (formerly ArmSEFF), EBRD has committed EUR 15 million for sustainable energy lending through commercial banks in Armenia. Loans are targeted at the following 3 sectors – SME, residential and renewable energy. Three banks are currently participating in the programme.
- *Azerbaijan:* As of the end of 2013, there was no SEFF in Azerbaijan, although EBRD extended a EUR 4.2 million loan in 2013 for energy efficiency improvements to the headquarters of AccessBank Azerbaijan.
- *Belarus:* EBRD has committed EUR 40 million for energy efficiency lending through commercial banks. Loans are targeted at the following 4 sectors – commercial, industrial, renewable energy and energy efficiency suppliers (working capital). Four banks are currently participating in the programme.
- *Georgia:* Branded as Energocredit, EBRD has committed EUR 35 million for residential and SME energy efficiency. A total of 4 banks are participating in the facility.
- *Moldova:* A credit line of EUR 40 million has been committed for SME lending (MoSEFF), through 5 partner banks, together with an additional EUR 35 million for residential energy efficiency (MoREEFF) through 4 partner banks.
- *Ukraine:* The Ukraine Energy Efficiency Programme (UKEEP) was established in 2007. It financed 77 projects with a total value of EUR 150 million. The focus is primarily on business energy efficiency, although renewable energy projects are also eligible. In 2013, the EBRD approved another USD 100 million credit line to extend UKEEP until 2016.
- *Russian Federation:* EBRD has committed EUR 150 million in corporate and EUR 75 million in residential energy efficiency credit lines through the RUSEFF programme.
- *In Central Asia:* In the Kyrgyz Republic, EBRD has committed EUR 15 million through the KyrSEFF facility for residential and small business lending. A further 2 credit lines were implemented in Kazakhstan in 2008-2009 to the value of EUR 29 million.

The banks that participate in SEFF operations tend to be those that already have a well-established relationship with EBRD. The majority have already undertaken a number of credit lines on more mainstream products (consumer finance, SME finance). In many countries in the region, the pool of available lenders with which the IFIs can engage is relatively small (reflecting their strict standards of governance, credit worthiness and transparency).

Table 3.2 provides an overview of the participating financial institutions in each country.

Table 3.2. **Overview of EBRD participating financial institutions in the EaP countries, Russia and Central Asia**

Country	Partner banks	SECTORS IN TARGET – Energy efficiency				Renewable energy
		Residential	SME	Corporate	Energy supplier	
ARM	▪ ACBA Bank ▪ Ameriabank ▪ SEF International	✓	✓			✓
AZE	▪ Access Bank			✓		
BLR	▪ MTB Bank ▪ Belgazprombank ▪ Belvnesheconombank ▪ BPS Sberbank		✓	✓ corporate and industrial	✓	✓
GEO	▪ Bank of Georgia ▪ TBC Bank ▪ Bank Republic (Société Générale) ▪ Credo	✓	✓	✓		
MDL	▪ Moldinconbank Chisinau MICB ▪ BCR ▪ Moldova Agroindbank - MAIB ▪ Mobiasbanca ▪ Procredit	✓	✓	✓		✓
UKR	▪ Ukreximbank ▪ MGB Megabank ▪ Raiffeisen Bank Aval		✓	✓		✓
RUS	▪ Rosbank ▪ Unicredit ▪ NDB Bank ▪ Bank Center Invest ▪ Bystrobank ▪ Orient Express Bank ▪ Asian Pacific Bank (APB) ▪ Botlease Eurasia ▪ Transcapitalbank (TCB)	✓		✓		
Central Asia	▪ Demir Bank ▪ Kyrgyz Investment and Credit Bank (KCB) ▪ Bai Tushum Bank ▪ Finca	✓		✓		

Source: Author's own work based on web review of relevant credit lines.

Figures 3.1 and 3.2 set out the evolution of the portfolio and the volume of lending by country. The volume of finance is greatest in the Russian Federation and Ukraine, with substantial lending operations in Moldova, Georgia and Belarus. This, to some extent, reflects the relative size of the market opportunity and the size of the banks (allowing for larger scale credit lines).

Figure 3.1. **EBRD SEFF loans in the EaP countries, Kyrgyzstan and Russia, 2006-2013, million EUR**

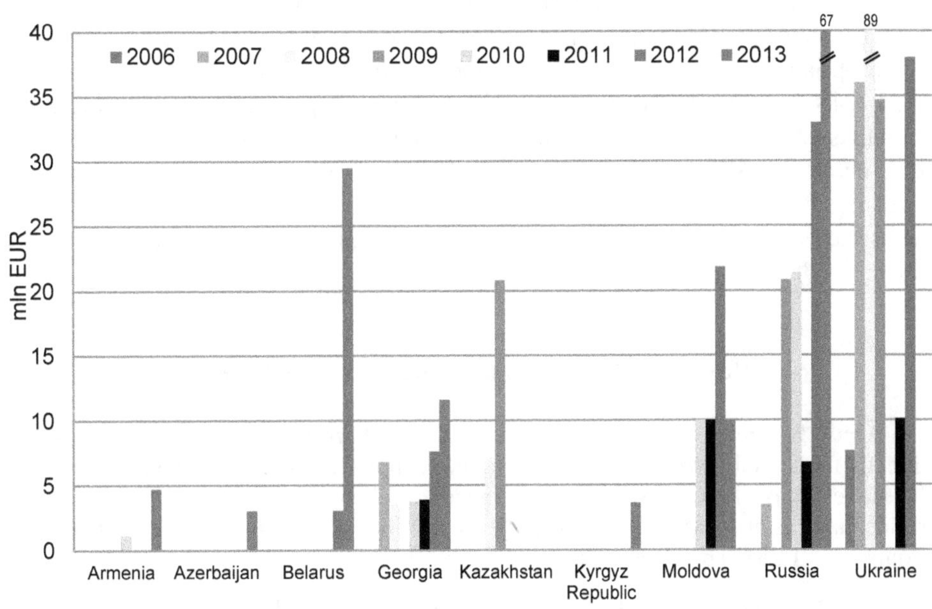

Note: The numbers represent SEFF lending to the national FIs, rather than the commitment made by the EBRD to the facility.

Source: Information provided by EBRD.

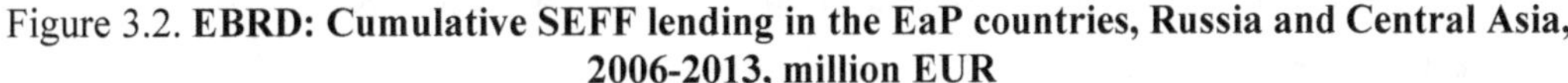

Figure 3.2. **EBRD: Cumulative SEFF lending in the EaP countries, Russia and Central Asia, 2006-2013, million EUR**

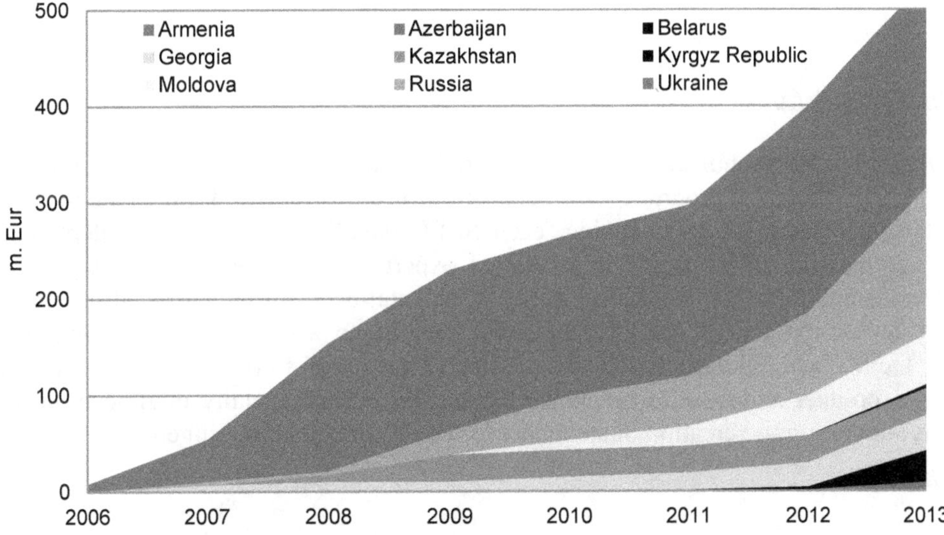

Note: The numbers represent SEFF lending to the national FIs, rather than the commitment made by the EBRD to the facility.

Source: Information provided by EBRD.

EBRD also participates in a multi-lateral facility that is supporting environmental finance through local financial institutions – Green for Growth Fund. This facility is explained separately later in the report.

Incentives to borrowers

EBRD operates on market based principles when negotiating credit lines with commercial banks in an attempt not to distort the wider market. However, donor funds, where appropriate, may be used to address specific barriers and market failures, mitigate perceived risks, provide tenor extensions, bridge capital gaps and provide performance fees to banks. As part of this approach, EBRD has structured a system of incentive payments across its SEFF facilities of 5% to 30% of the loan amount to end borrowers. The level is set based on market research prior to the facility launch and reflects the willingness of end borrowers to pay, and the level of prevailing regulatory support (e.g. fiscal incentives) to invest.

Box 3.1. **EBRD End user incentives: Armenia**

ArmSEFF credit lines are supported by an end borrower user incentive. This is paid directly to the end borrower by the bank using donor grant funds provided by EBRD. The incentive is available across the full range of client sectors (commercial, industrial, residential), as well as for eligible projects fulfilling the List of Eligible Materials and Equipment (LEME) requirements.

A standard cash payment of 10% is available to end borrowers upon implementation. This increases to 15% for companies undergoing an energy audit and subsequently implementing a recommended best available technology solution.

Incentive payments are not available for investments in renewable energy and for investments in their own premises by partner banks. Each Partner Bank has the right to design the Incentive Payment procedure according to its own loan processing rules.

Source: www.energocredit.am, accessed 10 September 2015.

Technical assistance

Donor funded technical assistance is provided free of charge to banks (and sub-borrowers) where appropriate to support project origination, development and monitoring. In addition to financing, each SEFF establishes a Project Implementation Team, comprising of local and international experts who provide support to financial institutions and their clients. The project implementation team will work at the national facility level supporting those local financial institutions who agree to participate in the SEFF facility and take an EBRD credit line. They train staff in promoting the new financial product and how to recognise technically and financially eligible projects as well as supporting the creation of standards for environmental due diligence.

Box 3.2. **EBRD eligibility criteria: Belarus**

BelSEFF credit lines are subject to a number of financial, environmental and technical screening criteria. Borrowers are subject to the following criteria:

- Borrowers may be either private sector companies registered in Belarus (including energy service companies (ESCOs) and leasing companies), or public sector companies, deemed creditworthy and implementing projects solely through a private sector contractor;
- Meet the participating bank's credit criteria and be approved in accordance with its credit appraisal procedures;
- Apply procurement rules in accordance with the EBRD's Procurement Policies and Rules (PPR);
- Be in compliance with the national environmental, health and safety and labour legislation in Belarus, or agree to address areas of non-compliance (as reflected in the project agreement);
- Not be engaged in activities listed on the EBRD Environmental Exclusion and Referral List;
- Not finance any environmentally or socially sensitive business activities listed on the EBRD Environmental and Social Referral List.

In addition, the following screening criteria are applied:

- Industrial and commercial buildings: minimum energy saving effect in terms of unit per output not less than 20% compared to the baseline;
- Stand-alone renewable energy projects: Positive Net Present Value calculated over a 10-year period using an 8% discount rate to the underlying cash flows denominated in hard currency.

For smaller scale projects (loans USD 400 000), approval can be given on the basis of the List of Eligible Measures and Equipment (LEME) and the List of Equipment Suppliers and Installers (LESI). This aims to simplify procedures for smaller energy efficiency projects. Together, these represent technologies capable of meeting the 20% energy savings, together with those companies having the required registration for supply and installation in Belarus.

Source: www.belseff.by, accessed 10 September 2015.

These experts also provide borrowers with support in identifying energy saving opportunities, developing financing applications, enhancing project design and advising on high performance technologies. The interaction between all parties involved in the credit line implementation is shown in Figure 3.3.

Figure 3.3. **Overview of EBRD support model**

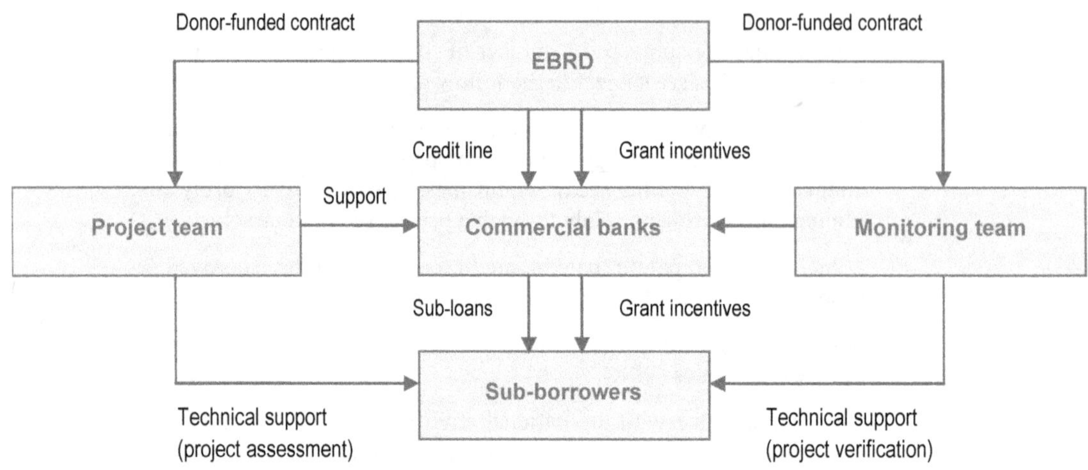

Source: EBRD (2013).

EBRD also engages in donor-funded policy dialogue in the region to help support the development of strong institutional and regulatory frameworks for energy efficiency and renewable energy. Examples include assisting the Governments of Moldova and the Kyrgyz Republic to transpose the EU Energy Performance of Buildings Directive, which has led to the development of dedicated buildings energy efficiency credit lines.

International Finance Corporation

The IFC has been implementing sustainable energy finance in the region through commercial banks since 2005. The initial focus was on the Russian Federation through the Russia Sustainable Energy Finance Program (RSEFP). More recently, lending activities have expanded into Armenia, Azerbaijan, Belarus and Ukraine. Credit lines are supported by donor funded technical assistance facilities.

Portfolio size and structure

In the Russian Federation, as of July 2012, more than USD 242 million had been issued through partner financial institutions, financing more than 270 energy efficiency projects in the SME sector[2]. Since 2010, sustainable energy and energy efficiency credit lines across the region (including the Russian Federation and Central Asia) have totalled more than USD 100 million, of which USD 44 million has been agreed with 6 banks in the EaP region. In 2008, the IFC also implemented a USD 20 million consumer residential EE credit line through Procredit Ukraine. Within the Clean Technology Fund (CTF) programme in Ukraine, IFC is currently projected to implement credit lines to the value of USD 85 million. These will be financed through USD 15 million of CTF funds, USD 60 million of IFC finance and USD 25 million of private sector co-financing. The loans will be targeted across a range of sectors (commercial, SME, residential). Negotiations are ongoing with local FIs and board approval was expected in Q2 2014. There are currently no dedicated lending facilities in Central Asia.[3]

Table 3.3 sets out the participating financial institutions for IFC credit lines.

Table 3.3. **IFC Partner Banks receiving energy efficiency credit lines in Armenia, Azerbaijan, Belarus, Russia and Ukraine**

Country	Partner Banks	SECTORS IN TARGET		
		Residential	SME	Corporate
ARM	▪ Ameriabank ▪ HSBC ▪ Byblos Bank	✓	✓	
AZE	▪ Bank Respublica			✓
BLR	▪ MTB		✓	
UKR	▪ Credit Europe		✓	
RUS	▪ Absolutbank ▪ Agropromcredit ▪ CBM ▪ Center Invest ▪ Delta Credit ▪ Independent Leasing ▪ LockoBank ▪ MDM Bank ▪ NDB Bank ▪ Prime Finance Bank ▪ Tatfondbank ▪ Transcapital Bank ▪ Ursa Bank	✓	✓	

Source: Information provided by IFC.

Figure 3.4 sets out the development of the IFC portfolio since 2010.

Figure 3.4. **IFC Sustainable energy finance portfolio in Armenia, Azerbaijan, Belarus, Russia and Ukraine, 2010 - 2014**

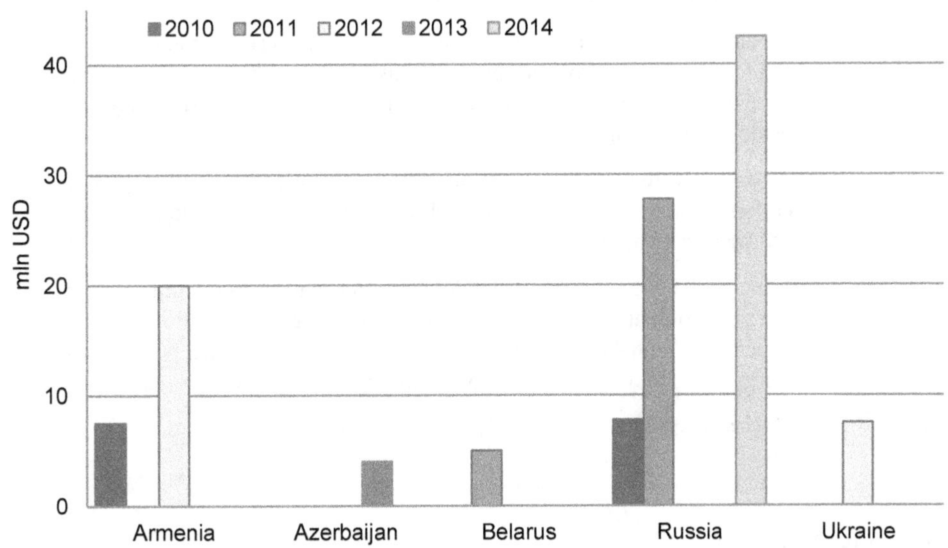

Source: Information provided by IFC.

The main focus of IFC lending has been in the SME and residential sectors (companies generally must be privately owned). For the SME sector, eligible technologies have included:

- Generic energy technologies (motors, combined heat and power generation, boiler equipment, compressors, lighting, etc.);
- Industrial process modernisation, resulting in lower energy consumption per unit of output;
- Renewable energy (where economically feasible).

Technologies must be approved and tested, and able to demonstrate a substantial energy efficiency effect, with a simple payback period of less than five years. Often, energy efficiency loans are bundled alongside more general SME loans. For example, MTB Bank Belarus received a USD 10 million credit line of which 50% was dedicated to SME energy efficiency lending.

Box 3.3. IFC Ukraine Residential Energy Efficiency Project

The IFC Ukraine Residential Energy Efficiency Project is designed to create an effective legal and institutional platform to support Ukrainian homeowner associations and housing management companies in obtaining access to finance for the energy-efficient modernisation of multifamily buildings. Through the project, IFC aims to facilitate energy efficiency investments in Ukraine's residential sector. The residential housing sector in Ukraine consumes approximately 25% of the country's electricity and 40% of its heat energy resources.

Some of the principal barriers to residential energy efficiency in Ukraine relate to the undeveloped status of homeowner associations, absence of targeted state support and lack of control over energy use. Other issues include regulated energy prices, the inability of financial institutions to lend to the sector because of contradictions in legislation concerning homeowner associations, and a lack of knowledge about the benefits of residential energy efficiency.

In Ukraine, in this context, the IFC also aims to:

- Develop legislation in close cooperation with government agencies to enable local homeowner associations and housing management companies to access finance to improve energy efficiency in residential buildings.
- Increase awareness about residential energy efficiency among key market stakeholders by relationship-building and development of information campaigns.
- Work with Ukrainian banks to develop and market financially viable energy efficient housing loan products targeted at homeowner associations and housing management companies for the purpose of energy efficiency renovations to multifamily buildings.

Source: www.ifc.org, accessed on 10 September 2015.

Incentives to borrowers

IFC policy is not to use concessional funds to distort the wider commercial lending market. It encourages FIs to lend on projects that have sufficient rates of return and payback periods without further recourse to subsidy. Where these rates of return could be improved through regulatory and economic reform, IFC will work with national governments to improve the enabling environment.

Technical assistance

In terms of technical assistance, IFC has used a combination of donor-funded in-house advisory teams, supported by external technical consultants, as appropriate. These teams have provided a full range of technical advisory to FIs in the development of EE lending products, pipeline development, project preparation, training and impact measurement.

The IFC has placed a strong focus on policy development support. A major example is the report prepared jointly with the World Bank which helped support the development of energy efficiency regulations in the Russian Federation (IFC 2008).

As Table 3.4 below sets out, advisory services (both in terms of policy support to governments and product support to individual financial institutions) tend to be established in a country prior to any credit lines being issued. In addition, the number of financial institutions receiving advisory support is higher than the number receiving finance, demonstrating the stand-alone value of energy efficiency advisory.

Table 3.4. **Provision of IFC Advisory Services in Europe and Central Asia region**

Country	Programme	Advisory legal / regulatory	Advisory preceded investment	# of FIs receiving advisory	IFC funding received
ARM	Sustainable energy finance	y	y	3	2
	Renewable Energy/Small hydro power plants	y	y	2	2
UKR	Sustainable energy finance	n	y	3	1
	Residential EE	y	y	2	1
RUS	Sustainable energy finance	y	y	12+3	5+2
	Residential EE	y	y	2	1

Note: y – Yes, n – No.

Source: Information provided by IFC.

In respect of the thematic areas, energy efficiency and renewable energy credit lines are supported in parallel by a range of donor funded technical assistance (TA) facilities:

- *Sustainable Energy Finance Programmes:* These TA facilities are donor financed, and provide a wide range of advisory services to financial institutions, their clients, and other market players to support investments in energy efficiency and renewable energy. IFC helps financial institutions to develop local expertise in energy efficiency-based lending through training seminars, joint promotional activities, resource materials, and advice on transactions. The programmes also assist end-user companies to analyse energy efficiency projects under consideration and identify opportunities to save energy. Support is also given to help vendors and product developers build relationships with potential clients and financial institutions. The choice of banks to receive advisory services support is determined by a combination of the position of the FI in the market (volume, profile), together with the likelihood of the FI agreeing to receive IFC finance. Where appropriate, wider policy and market development support is provided through the undertaking of market surveys, such as those published in the EaP region (IFC, 2010a). The programmes also engage in awareness raising and public policy work to overcome barriers to investment. Programmes are ongoing in the Russian Federation, Armenia and Ukraine.

- *Resource Efficiency Programmes:* Similar advisory service programmes are underway in the area of broader resource efficiency operating at the firm, sector and policy level. These target a wider range of water and waste. For example, the Ukraine programme has worked with the government on the development of a Green Tariff proposal supporting businesses to access feed-in tariffs.
- *Residential Energy Efficiency Project:* The Ukraine Residential Energy Efficiency Project is working with the Government of Ukraine to develop energy efficiency legislation, increase awareness and develop housing loan products for residential blocks.
- *Europe and Central Asia (ECA) Cleaner Production Programme:* IFC also operates a cleaner production programme, targeting 3-5 companies per year in the Russian Federation and Ukraine through a combination of advisory and investment products. Technical support includes scoping studies, co-financing of cleaner production audits, and implementation support for eligible projects. Alongside dedicated financing for large industrial and municipal enterprises, the programme will also extend credit lines to local financial institutions for on-lending purposes. IFC aims to facilitate over USD 90 million in market-priced financing for cleaner production investments, which are expected to result in the avoidance/or the reduction of at least 120 000 tons/year of greenhouse gas emissions. The programme also supports the raising of awareness among policy makers and financial institutions through the undertaking of sectoral benchmarking, market studies, best practice and Best Available Techniques (BAT) guidelines, production of case studies and conducting seminars for company managers and technical specialists.
- *Resource Efficiency in Nitrogen-Based Chemical and Fertilizer Production Benchmarking Project:* Implemented in the Russian Federation, Ukraine and Central Asia, the project aims to undertake benchmarking in the fertiliser sector that compares specific indicators related to production inputs and emissions with the analogical average and best industry values, thereby revealing areas for improvement and cost savings.

Table 3.5. **IFC Advisory Services Programmes in Europe and Central Asia region**

Programme	ARM	AZE	BLR	GEO	MDL	UKR	RUS	Central Asia
Sustainable Energy Finance Program	✓		✓			✓	✓	
ECA Resource Efficiency Program	✓	✓	✓	✓	✓	✓	✓	✓
Fertiliser resource efficiency benchmarking project	✓	✓	✓	✓		✓	✓	✓
Residential Energy Efficiency Project						✓		
Cleaner Production Programme						✓	✓	

Source: Information provided by IFC.

European Investment Bank

Since October 2011, climate change mitigation and adaptation have represented one of the three main pillars for lending for EIB, alongside SME/private sector, and social and economic infrastructure. Intermediated loans through local financial institutions are normally the preferred route for investments under EUR 25 million.

To date, EIB environmental lending through local financial institutions (FIs) in the EaP and neighbouring countries has been done primarily through SME loans. Some of these loans allow for FIs to disburse up to a specific limit for energy and environment purposes alongside their primary designation. However, there is no minimum requirement for this to be the case, and loans can be used purely for SME or other mandated uses at the discretion of the local FI.

In Kazakhstan, the EIB is beginning implementation of 3 projects with a specific climate change focus:

- EUR 120 million credit line to the Development Bank of Kazakhstan. There is a minimum 30% allocation for climate action (both mitigation and adaptation) under the EIB Climate Action mandate (covering both mitigation and adaptation);
- EUR 100 million credit line to Sberbank Kazakhstan for SMEs and Midcaps. There is a minimum 30% allocation for climate action (both mitigation and adaptation) under the EIB Climate Action mandate (covering both mitigation and adaptation);
- EUR 150 million dedicated EIB loan to finance climate change projects to Kazagro will target the agri-food sector in Kazakhstan, promoted by rural micro, small and medium-sized enterprises (MSMEs), SMEs and mid-caps. The loan will focus on financing projects contributing to climate change adaptation, such as resource efficiency (e.g. water efficiency, irrigation), protection of soil erosion schemes (buffer zones, river bank fencing), improved logistics and grain elevators, afforestation of degraded land, and possibly climate mitigation (e.g. biomass energy projects).

EIB also participates in two multi-lateral facilities that are supporting environmental debt finance – Green for Growth and the Global Climate Partnership Fund. These facilities are explained separately below.

Within the EaP region, there have been no targeted energy efficiency technical assistance programmes alongside SME credit lines. Where energy and environmental lending is permitted, but not mandated, borrowers have been provided with EIB list of Climate Action definitions deployed by the EIB for the purposes of awareness and compliance. This model is due to change for the Kazakhstan operations where there is a minimum Climate Action component. The TA element to support Kazakh lending operations will be funded under the Investment Facility for Central Asia[4] which provides EU grant support for technical assistance packages and concessional finance alongside IFI loans. External consultancy support will be provided to offer training, capacity building, project origination, screening and reporting services to the partner local financial institutions.

Table 3.6 sets out EIB activities which may have an explicit or implicit environmental orientation, but are not dedicated energy efficiency or renewable energy loans in the sense understood by EBRD or IFC. Projects in fields considered as priority (including climate change mitigation and adaptation) carried out by eligible promoters of any size can also be funded, provided that financing thereto does not exceed 30% of the overall EIB loan amount.

Table 3.6. **EIB SME loans with potential environmental component**

Country	Year	Loan	mln EUR	Comments
ARM	2013	Green for Growth II	3.75	
	2011	ProCredit Holdings loan for SME and Priority Projects A	15	
AZE	2013	Green for Growth II	1.25	
GEO	2013	Green for Growth II	3.75	
	2010	Société Générale SME and Energy/Environment Loan	35	
	2011	ProCredit Holdings loan for SME and Priority Projects A	15	
	2012	TCB Bank for SME and Energy/Environment Loan	25	
	2012	ProCredit Holdings loan for SME and Priority Projects A	10	
MDL	2013	Green for Growth II	1.25	
	2013	Mobiasbanka loan for SME and Mid caps	20	
	2011	ProCredit Holdings loan for SME and Priority Projects A	20	
	2010	Société Générale SME and Energy/Environment Loan	20	
KAZ	2013	Kazagro Climate loan for MSMEs, SMEs and Mid Caps	150	*Covered by EIB Guarantee*
	2013	Development Bank of Kazakhstan Climate Loan and SME loan	120	*Covered by EIB Guarantee. Min 30% for Climate action*
	2013	Sberbank Kazakhstan SME and Mid Cap Loan	100	*Min 30% for Climate action*
RUS	2013	VTB (Foreign Trade Bank) loan for SME and mid-caps	200	
	2013	Unicredit loan for SME and mid caps	100	
	2013	Raiffeisen Bank Loan for SME and mid caps	40	
	2013	VEB Entrepreneurship Fund for SMEs and mid-caps	113	
	2013	VEB SME and mid-caps	200	
	2013	Sberbank SME and mid-caps	300	
UKR	2013	Green for Growth II	2.5	
	2013	Oschadbank	220	
	2012	Prominvestbank SME and midcaps	200	
	2012	Ukreximbank SME and mid-caps	100	
	2009	Forumbank SME and Energy/Environment Loan	100	
	2012	Unicredit	140	
Regional	2013	GEEREF (Global Energy Efficiency and Renewable Energy Fund)	1.1	*Regional contribution*
	2014	Global Climate Partnership Fund (KfW, IFC)	60	*Global*

Note: Many of these lending facilities have the option of lending to energy and environment projects, but have no minimum target. Although the authors are aware that some of the facilities have been used to finance environmental projects, they have not been included in the overall total estimates of lending.

Source: Information provided by EIB.

World Bank (IBRD)

The IBRD acts primarily as a lender to state-owned financial institutions, with IFC providing the main World Bank Group point of contact for commercial banks. Finance for environmental purposes tends to be targeted at state-owned organisations, and is delivered through government agencies.

There are a limited number of examples of the IBRD working with state-owned banks to develop environmental credit lines. For example:

- In Ukraine, IBRD signed a USD 200 million credit line with Ukreximbank in 2011. The credit line was supported by a sovereign guarantee, and had a 6-year grace period. The purpose is to improve energy efficiency of industrial and commercial companies, municipalities, municipal sector enterprises and energy service companies. Commercial debt financing and equity co-financing will be drawn on to co-finance projects; additional grant co-funding may also become available through potential future climate finance and the Eastern European energy efficiency and environment partnership. The borrower will also on-lend to other eligible financial institutions – participating banks – that are willing to invest in eligible energy efficiency projects in the industrial and municipal sector. This will improve the capacity of local financial institutions to identify and evaluate potential energy efficiency investments. As of December 2013, 5 sub-loans had been agreed, and negotiations were on-going with 2 participating banks. Approximately USD 43 million had been disbursed, generating estimated energy savings of 147 GWh against a target of 400 GWh.
- In the Russian Federation, IBRD is negotiating a concessional USD 300 million credit line with the state owned bank Vnesheconombank, supported by a USD 25 million grant facility funded by the Global Environmental Facility. This will be on lent to clients. No further details are yet available.

In terms of policy support, reform activities are sometimes supported through development policy loans with an energy and environment reform component. This was done, for example, in Ukraine, in 2007. In addition, the World Bank implements a number of dedicated energy policy support projects. An example is the Energy Efficiency Project for Armenia (USD 10.6 million), including capacity building support for the national R2E2 Energy Efficiency Fund.

Asian Development Bank

Within the EaP countries, the Asian Development Bank (ADB) has operations in the Caucasus, and elsewhere in Central Asia. In the Caucasus, ADB promotes SME finance through local financial institutions, but does not offer dedicated environmental credit lines.

In Central Asia, one credit line has been identified.

In Tajikistan, the Access to Green Finance Project seeks to use the country's microfinance system to provide credit for households and microenterprises for energy efficient and environment-friendly homes. The grant will comprise project implementation support of USD 1.2 million and USD 8.8 million for 5-year, local currency denominated credit lines to selected microfinance institutions (MFIs). The interest rate on the credit lines will be the National Bank of Tajikistan refinancing rate, reset annually. An additional technical assistance grant of USD 750 000, provided by the Japan Fund for Poverty Reduction, will build the capacity of MFIs and the project management unit to facilitate efficient green finance intermediation and promote energy efficiency in the country, particularly for rural households and women. The Ministry of Finance will lend USD 8.8 million to MFIs for energy efficient and environmentally friendly solutions. The MFIs will provide credits (up to USD 5 000) to households and microenterprises for solar home solutions, energy efficient cook stoves and heat exchanger units, home insulation solutions.

There are also a number of policy oriented TA initiatives, such as the Uzbekistan Solar Energy Development Project, and support to the Pilot Project for Climate Resilience in Tajikistan.

NEFCO

The Nordic Environment Finance Corporation (NEFCO) is an international finance institution established by the five Nordic countries. NEFCO finances investments and projects primarily in the Russian Federation, Ukraine, Estonia, Latvia, Lithuania, Moldova and Belarus. NEFCO tends to lend directly through a number of directly operated facilities, rather than through financial institutions. Under the Facility for Energy Saving Projects (EUR 12.4 million) and the Facility for Cleaner Production (EUR 14.8 million), NEFCO offers direct project financing for public and private entities in the Russian Federation, Ukraine and Belarus. The repayment of the loan is directly tied to the energy and financial savings of the investment. The Investment Fund (EUR 113 million) provides direct support to environmentally beneficial projects.

A number of environmental credit lines have been facilitated by NEFCO through these products. Examples include:

- NEFCO set up a joint facility with Bank Lviv in 2008 in Ukraine to promote energy efficiency investments. Bank Lviv is owned by international investors. The facility lends on small scale projects for energy efficiency improvements. EUR 3 million has been lent to more than 1 400 households and 6 companies for energy efficiency improvements. Most of the finance has been used to pay for windows, boilers and heat exchangers. Buildings-scale renewables are also financed (solar, biomass boilers). Loan amounts range from UAH 30-100 000 with a repayment period of 36 months. The project has reduced 16 000 MWh per annum and reduced CO_2 emissions by 22 000 tons.
- In Belarus, in 2013, NEFCO provided EUR 1.5 million from the Investment Fund to support a facility in the Belarus National Bank to renew trucks. The new facility is expected to stimulate demand for trucks with lower fuel consumption, which in turn will bring environmental benefits in the form of reduced emissions of carbon dioxide, nitrogen oxides, carbon monoxide and black carbon. The main focus will be on trucks, which meet the so-called euro-5 emissions standards.[5]
- In 2014, NEFCO announced it would contribute EUR 3 million from its Investment Fund to a new facility with Minsk Transit Bank (MTBank) in Belarus to support energy efficiency projects for the bank's current and potential customers. Energy savings of at least 25% are expected.

Donor development banks

Two donor development banks, providing environmental credit lines to the EaP countries, have been identified for this analysis. These include the German KfW and the Austrian Development Bank.

KfW

KfW of Germany has implemented 4 credit lines in the EaP countries.

Table 3.7. **KfW environmental credit lines in Armenia, Georgia and Ukraine, 2004 - 2012**

Year	Country	Value	Bank	Sector
2012	Georgia	EUR 25 mln	Bank of Georgia	RE
2010	Armenia	EUR 18 mln	GAF	RE
2008	Ukraine	USD 30 mln	Procredit	SME/EE
2004	Armenia	EUR 6 mln	GAF	RE

In 2008, a credit line of USD 30 million was provided to Procredit in Ukraine (in which KfW is a major shareholder) for the development of an SME energy efficiency product. This was supported by a technical consultancy contract to support the design and implementation. Procredit had previously received financing from IFC for its ProRemont Eco product aimed at the residential sector.

In Georgia and Armenia, there are a set of credit lines for the development of renewable energy, primarily small hydropower.

In Georgia, a EUR 25 million loan to Bank of Georgia (supported by a EUR 0.75 million technical assistance package, co-financed by the Austrian Development Bank) was agreed in 2012. The facility, with a maturity of 10 years, is mainly being used to provide long term loan finance for the construction or rehabilitation of small size hydropower plants up to 20 MW.

In Armenia, KfW has provided EUR 24 million over 2 phases (EUR 6 million in 2004 and EUR 18 million in 2010) to the German-Armenian Fund (a unit of the Armenian Central Bank), which is on-lending the funds to private Armenian banks for financing of small hydropower plants of up to 10 MW.

Other credit lines are only in the planning phase. KfW also participates in the Green for Growth Fund, with some additional activities financed through the Global Climate Partnership Fund (GCPF). Further details are set out below.

Austrian Development Bank

The Austrian Development Bank (OEDB) has recently implemented a number of environmental lending operations in the Russian Federation and the Caucasus. The credit lines in the Caucasus are combined SME/EE operations. These are set out in Table 3.8 as follows:

Table 3.8. **OEDB environmental credit lines in Armenia, Georgia and Russia, 2012 - 2013**

Year	Country	Value	Bank	Sector
2013	Georgia	USD 15 mln	Procredit	SME/EE
	Armenia	USD 15 mln	Ameriabank	SME/EE
2012	Russia	EUR 20 mln	Center Invest	SME/EE

OEDB also supports a range of relevant technical advisory and risk-sharing facilities in the Caucasus. These include financing the UNIDO/UNEP National Cleaner Production Center in Georgia, and a risk facility for a KfW loan supporting small hydropower development through the Bank of Georgia.

Multilateral finance instruments

Three multilateral finance instruments have been reviewed for this analysis. These include: the Green for Growth Fund, the Global Climate Partnership Fund and the Eastern Europe Energy Efficiency and Environment Partnership.

Green for Growth Fund

Initiated in December 2009 by the KfW and EIB with the financial support of the European Commission and EBRD, the Green for Growth Fund (GGF) Southeast Europe is dedicated to enhancing energy efficiency and fostering renewable energies in Southeast Europe, including Albania, Bosnia and Herzegovina, Croatia, FYR Macedonia, Kosovo, Montenegro, Serbia and Turkey as well as in the nearby EaP countries. The GGF provides refinancing to financial institutions for on-lending to enterprises and private households for energy efficiency projects. The GGF also invests directly in specialist energy service companies (ESCOs) as well as energy service and supply companies, and renewable energy projects. The activities of the GGF are supported by a Technical Assistance Facility. The GGF is a public-private partnership with an investor base of donor agencies, international financial institutions and institutional private investors. The GGF is privately managed by Oppenheim Asset Management, in concert with the fund advisor, Finance in Motion GmbH, Frankfurt/Main, Germany, and a technical advisor, MACS Management & Consulting Services GmbH, Frankfurt/Main, Germany.

The Fund has made 5 investments to date in the EaP countries, four in Armenia and one in Ukraine. These are as shown in Table 3.9 below.

Table 3.9. **Green for Growth credit lines in Armenia and Ukraine, 2012 - 2013**

Country	Year	Financial institution	Credit line	Projected energy savings	Projected GHG avoidance	Sector
			Mln EUR	*MWh/year*	*$tCO_2e/year$*	
ARM	2013	ACBA	3.629	na	na	Residential, MSME
		ACBA Leasing	1.725	na	na	Residential, MSME
	2012	Inecobank	10	36 000	8 200	Residential, MSME
		Araratbank	5	19 580	4 392	Residential, MSME
UKR	2012	Megabank	10	26 000	6 100	Corporate, SME, Industry

Source: http://www.ggf.lu, accessed 15 September 2015.

The Fund monitors achieved savings in primary energy and CO_2 emissions at the level of the FI loan and sub-loan. The management consortium uses eSave, a tool for calculation, monitoring and reporting of RE/EE measures and credit portfolios. Energy types such as final or useful energy are converted into primary energy before being reported. Similarly, the calculation of CO_2 savings is based on the individual specifications of each underlying project. Such details include the national grid emission factor[6], climate conditions and solar irradiation.

Global Climate Partnership Fund

The Global Climate Partnership Fund (GCPF) is a partnership between IFC, EIB and KfW. It seeks to provide debt focusing on small scale energy efficiency and renewable energy investments, either directly or via local financial institutions. It is a global fund targeting energy intensive economies, of which Ukraine is one.

The GCPF disbursed USD 30 million to the State Export-Import Bank of Ukraine (Ukreximbank) under a seven year senior unsecured loan facility[7]. The funding provided to Ukreximbank shall be used to refinance investments in energy efficiency measures as well as renewable energy production. Projects to be refinanced cover a broad range and include *inter alia* investments in the insulation of buildings, lightening modernisation or efficiency improvements of ventilation and heating systems. Ukreximbank targets small and medium enterprises as project owners while improvements of power generation facilities or the modernisation of production facilities of larger corporates may be included. Ukreximbank's strategy to support sustainable investments in the energy and SME sector provides a good fit with the investment targets of GCPF which – amongst others – has the goal to reduce CO_2 emissions by 20% on average across all energy efficiency measures.

Eastern Europe Energy Efficiency and Environment Partnership

The Eastern Europe Energy Efficiency and Environment Partnership (E5P) Fund is a EUR 90 million multi-donor fund managed by the EBRD designed to promote energy efficiency investments in Ukraine and other Eastern European countries and was set up under the initiative of the Swedish government during its presidency of the European Union in 2009. The fund complements energy efficiency loans provided by finance institutions, including EBRD, EIB, the Nordic Investment Bank, NEFCO and the World Bank Group. Grants under E5P will be allocated to four priority areas: district heating, other energy efficiency projects, environment projects in Ukraine as well as additional projects in other Eastern European countries. Armenia, Georgia and Moldova joined the Partnership in late 2013.

For comparative reasons, Table 3.10 provides an overview of the local banks that have worked with the IFIs on disbursing environmentally-related credit lines in the EECCA countries. IFIs have worked with and extended environmental credit lines to about 70 banks in the region, some of which have contracted more than one credit line. This approach offers capacity-building opportunities to a larger number of local FIs. Clearly, Russian and Ukrainian banks make up for about half of these, with Ukreximbank holding the largest number of IFI-supported credit lines in the region.

Table 3.10. **Overview of participating banks in the EaP counties, Russia and Central Asia**

	EBRD	IFC	EIB	World Bank	KfW	OEDB	NEFCO	GGF	GCPF
Armenia									
ACBA Bank	✓							✓	
Ameriabank	✓	✓				✓			
SEF International	✓								
HSBC		✓							
Byblos Bank		✓							
Procredit			✓						
Inecobank								✓	
Araratbank								✓	
German Armenian Fund*					✓				
Azerbaijan									
Access Bank	✓								
Bank Respublica		✓							
Belarus									
MTB Bank	✓	✓					✓		
Belgazprombank	✓								
Belvnesheconombank	✓								
BPS Sberbank	✓								
Belarus National Bank	✓						✓		
Georgia									
Bank of Georgia	✓				✓				
TBC Bank	✓		✓						
Bank Republic (Société Générale)	✓		✓						
Credo	✓								
Procredit	✓		✓			✓			
Moldova									
Moldinconbank Chisinau MICB	✓								
BCR	✓								
Moldova Agroindbank - MAIB	✓								
Mobiasbanca	✓		✓						
Procredit	✓		✓						
Ukraine									
Ukreximbank	✓		✓	✓					✓
MGB Megabank	✓							✓	
Raiffeisen Bank Aval	✓								
Credit Europe		✓							
Oschadbank			✓						
Prominvestbank			✓						
Forumbank			✓						
Unicredit			✓						
Procredit		✓			✓				
Bank Lviv							✓		
Russia									
Rosbank	✓								
Unicredit	✓		✓						
NDB Bank	✓	✓				✓			
Bank Center Invest	✓	✓							
Bystrobank	✓								
Orient Express Bank	✓								
Asian Pacific Bank (APB)	✓								
Botlease Eurasia	✓								

	EBRD	IFC	EIB	World Bank	KfW	OEDB	NEFCO	GGF	GCPF
Russia - Continued									
Transcapitalbank (TCB)	✓	✓							
Absolutbank		✓							
Agropromcredit		✓							
CBM		✓							
Delta Credit		✓							
Independent Leasing		✓							
LockoBank		✓							
MDM Bank		✓							
Prime Finance Bank		✓							
Tatfondbank		✓							
Ursa Bank		✓							
VTB			✓						
Raiffeisen Bank			✓						
VEB			✓	✓					
Sberbank			✓						
Central Asia									
Demir Bank	✓								
Kyrgyz Investment and Credit Bank (KCB)	✓								
Bai Tushum Bank	✓								
Finca	✓								
Development Bank of Kazakhstan			✓						
Sberbank Kazakhstan			✓						
Kazargo			✓						

Note: (*) German Armenian Fund is a unit of the Armenian Central Bank which on-lends to private banks to finance Small Hydro Plants projects. At present, there are 16 local partner FIs engaged with the programme.

Endnotes

1. These figures exclude EIB lending operations where there is a blended SME/Environment loan, with no minimum target for energy or environment, although we are aware that some of these funds have been used for on-lending to energy efficiency and renewable energy type projects.

2. RSEFP website (Accessed 21/04/2014) www.ifc.org/wps/wcm/connect/regprojects_ext_content/ifc_external_corporate_site/rsefp_home/achievements/achievements

3. A planned USD 21 million IFC programme in Kazakhstan on energy efficiency financing through financial intermediaries under the Clean Technology Fund was cancelled in 2010.

4. www.eib.org/projects/regions/central-asia/technical_assistance_and_grants/

5. Euro 5 standards refer to emission limits imposed by the European Union on pollution caused by road vehicles. These standards are specified in Regulation (EC) No 715/2007 of the European Parliament and of the Council of 20 June 2007. The Regulation aims to introduce stricter limits on pollutant emissions from light road vehicles that run on diesel, petrol, natural gas or Liquefied Petroleum Gas (LPG), particularly for emissions of nitrogen particulates and oxides.

6. A grid emission factor represents the greenhouse gas intensity of the national power grid as measured in tons of CO2 equivalent per MWh.

7. Senior debt takes priority over other unsecured or otherwise more "junior" debt. Unsecured refers to the fact that the loan is not secured against collateral.

References

Belarus Sustainable Energy Finance Facility, www.belseff.by

Clean Technology Fund (2013a), *Investment Plan for Ukraine*. Revision note, August 2013, www.climateinvestmentfunds.org

Climate Investment Funds (2013b), *Update of CTF Investment Plan for Kazakhstan,* www.climateinvestmentfunds.org

EBRD (2013), *Introduction to EBRD's Sustainable Energy Initiative*. Presentation to the first Berlin climate finance workshop, 25th February 2013

EBRD (2008), *Index of Sustainable Energy – Scores and Methodology*, EBRD, London, www.ebrd.com/downloads/research/brochures/isescores.pdf

IFC (2010a), *Energy Efficiency: A New Resource for Sustainable Growth. Researching Energy Efficiency Practices among Companies in Armenia, Azerbaijan, Belarus, Georgia, Russia and Ukraine,* IFC, Washington DC

IFC (2010b), *Russia Sustainable Energy Finance Facility Brochure* (Russian), IFC, Washington DC, www.ifc.org/wps/wcm/connect/96e800804b5f682389e0b96eac26e1c2/RSEFP_leaflet_Russian.pdf?MOD=AJPERES

IFC (2008), *Energy Efficiency in Russia: Untapped Reserves*, IFC, Washington DC, www.ifc.org/wps/wcm/connect/400e24004b5f69148d21bd6eac26e1c2/Final_EE_report_engl.pdf?MOD=AJPERES

KfW (2008), *Energy Efficiency Credit Lines: A proposal by KfW,* presentation available: www.energy-community.org/pls/portal/docs/174181.PDF

World Bank (2011), *Project Appraisal Document on a Proposed Loan in the Amount of US$200 Million to the Ukreximbank with the Guarantee of Ukraine for the Energy Efficiency Project*, World Bank, Washington DC, www.eximb.com/img/app_links/1245.pdf

Chapter 4.

Regulatory environment and transparency of information

Regulations require that both International Finance Institutions (IFIs) and local banks closely monitor and report on the environmental impact of their lending operations. This chapter discusses issues related to transparency of commercial and performance information associated with IFIs' portfolios of environmental credit lines. It also looks at how the lack of sufficiently available information can constrain the better understanding of some of the barriers to increased environmental lending in the EU's Eastern Partnership (EaP) countries.

IFI and local bank procedures

When setting up environmental credit lines, IFIs design *ex-ante* environmental targets and indicators against which the performance of the credit lines is evaluated during the *ex-post* monitoring process.

Ex-ante targets and indicators

IFIs broadly use *ex-ante* indicators for expected energy savings, renewable energy capacity installed and associated greenhouse gas (GHG) mitigation benefits during project design and approval phase. These are then tracked against actual impacts during implementation. This data is not normally publically available, other than in a consolidated form as part of regional or facility level reporting. In some cases, *ex-ante* targets will be reported. For example, the International Finance Corporation (IFC) Armenia Sustainable Energy Finance programme identifies the following *ex-ante* targets[1]:

- 35-megawatts of new renewable power generation capacity installed by 2015;
- A 120-gigawatt hours per year increase in renewable energy generation by 2015;
- 70 000 tons of greenhouse gas emissions avoided per year; and
- 20-gigawatt hours in annual energy savings.

Generally, *ex-ante* performance data is presented prior to board approval of a given loan or technical assistance project.

In terms of tracking, IFIs may also monitor non-performing loans (NPLs) among other indicators. This information is made available by local financial institutions with the support of external consultants and calculator tools, but is not publically available.

Ex-post monitoring processes

IFIs generally will undertake a review of project impact as part of a project closure report. However, many credit lines will not be subject to further *ex-post* monitoring with a view to understanding whether lending operations were successful in creating sustainable lending products.

Often, the IFIs have close relationships with their client banks in the EU's Eastern Partnership (EaP) countries as they are drawn from a small pool of eligible institutions that meet IFI lending criteria. Most will have multiple products with a single institution allowing them a form of informal monitoring. An IFI may also make repeat loans to a financial institution for energy efficiency purposes which extends the relationship period before which *ex-post* evaluation might be undertaken.

Energy efficiency credit lines may be reviewed as part of a sector evaluation process. The European Bank for Reconstruction and Development (EBRD), for example, has undertaken a number of evaluations of its Sustainable Energy Finance Facilities (SEFF). These, however, are not in the public domain.

Credit line structure

In addition to environmental impacts that have to be achieved through the credit lines, IFIs also need to monitor and report on various elements of the credit line structure. These include, among others, information on the end borrow profile, types of investments made, the leverage effect of the credit line as well as donor and other public funds used alongside the credit line. The commercial terms between the IFI and the FI and the on-lending terms are considered commercial in confidence and are not publically reported.

End borrower profile

The general profile of end borrowers is available for all of the credit lines identified (e.g. small and medium sized enterprises (SME), residential). Some have eligibility criteria associated in terms of private vs. public sector borrowers. However, the distribution by industry sector, size or turnover of the local financing institution (FI) portfolio is not usually reported in the public domain.

Type of investments made

All of the credit lines set out a list of eligibility criteria for minimum efficiency standards that must be achieved or technologies than can be financed. The actual profile of type of equipment bought as a result of the credit line is not usually reported in detail. Case studies are often provided which offer illustrative examples.

Commercial terms: IFI – FI

For most of the IFIs, the terms of the loans (tenor, interest rate, repayment conditions) between IFI and local financial institution (FI) are considered commercial in confidence and are not publically reported.

Occasionally, the general terms of lending are reported in IFI documents. For example, Box 5 sets out KfW's general approach to its energy efficiency facilities in South East Europe.

Box 4.1. **Example of commercial terms of energy efficiency lending products: KfW**

KfW energy efficiency lending products tend to be between EUR 10-15 million with terms and conditions depending on KfW's risk assessment. They have a maturity of up to 7 years with grace periods of up to 2 years. Interest rates may be fixed or floating. The margin is based on risk assessment, but usually reflects slightly reduced interest rates. Management and commitment fees are at market rates. Customary bank securities are required, and repayment is on a 6-month basis. Tailor made technical assistance is provided.

Source: www.energy-community.org/pls/portal/docs/174181.PDF, accessed on 10 September 2015.

On-lending terms: FI – End borrower

IFIs do not usually become involved in the commercial terms associated with the loans offered by intermediary financial institutions. The rate, tenor and any collateral conditions required by the bank are based on existing lending practices. EBRD, for example, provides end borrowers with an incentive payment, rather than seek to influence the cost or terms of finance offered by the intermediary banks. Where IFIs provide some level of concessionality in the loan terms, this may flow as a benefit to the local financial institution, rather than the end borrower, particularly where default levels are lower than those anticipated by the local financial institutions.

Leverage

Leverage is not clearly reported (either domestic or international), although tracked by some of the IFIs where local financial institutions commit some of their own funds. Sometimes, energy efficiency credit lines will be issued alongside more general SME credit lines and blended for the purposes of on-lending. Some banks use multiple FIs to finance their energy efficiency facilities. For example, Ameriabank (Armenia) has been the recipient of energy efficiency credit lines from at least three IFIs (EBRD, IFC, Austrian Development Bank).

Donor grants and other public funds

All of the IFIs use donor grants to support their technical assistance programmes, primarily consultant and facility support. Some information on the size and scope of these funds is publically available. EBRD uses grant funds to support end user incentive payments, although the total value of these payments is not publically available and may be blended with other technical assistance (TA) activity budgets. IFC occasionally uses concessional funds, for example in Armenia, alongside one of its credit lines (e.g. HSBC Armenia). Table 4.1 sets out EBRD's use of donor funds in support of sustainable energy lending.

Table 4.1. **EBRD use of donor funds**

Technical consultancy	Non-technical consultancy
Market demand studies	Sub-borrower incentives
Project consultants	Partner FI incentives
Verification consultants	Risk sharing
Assistance with policy dialogue	
Every 1 EUR spent on technical cooperation (TC) leads to EUR 83 of sustainable energy investments	*Every 1 EUR spent on Non-TC leads to EUR 6.3 of sustainable energy investment*

Source: EBRD (2013).

Credit line performance

To evaluate the performance of their credit lines IFIs usually consider two main criteria: the environmental impact of the credit line and the level of non-performing loans.

Environmental impact: Energy saving and CO_2 data

All IFIs now collect this data as part of the loan agreement, either from the banks, or through the use of technical consultants. Both EBRD and IFC have developed dedicated calculators with which to support the calculation of these savings. Occasionally, *ex-ante* estimates of CO_2 benefits will be disclosed as part of a public project document. Otherwise, this data is consolidated into regional reporting data.

For example, EBRD has provided the following aggregated performance data for the full Sustainable Energy Finance Facility (SEFF) loan portfolio for the EaP countries plus the Russian Federation and Central Asia. Currently, the portfolio is delivering annual energy savings of 2 400 000 MWh/year, resulting in GHG emissions reductions of more than 500 000 tCO_2e.

Figure 4.1. **Energy and CO_2 avoidance savings for SEFF in the EaP countries, Russia and Central Asia**

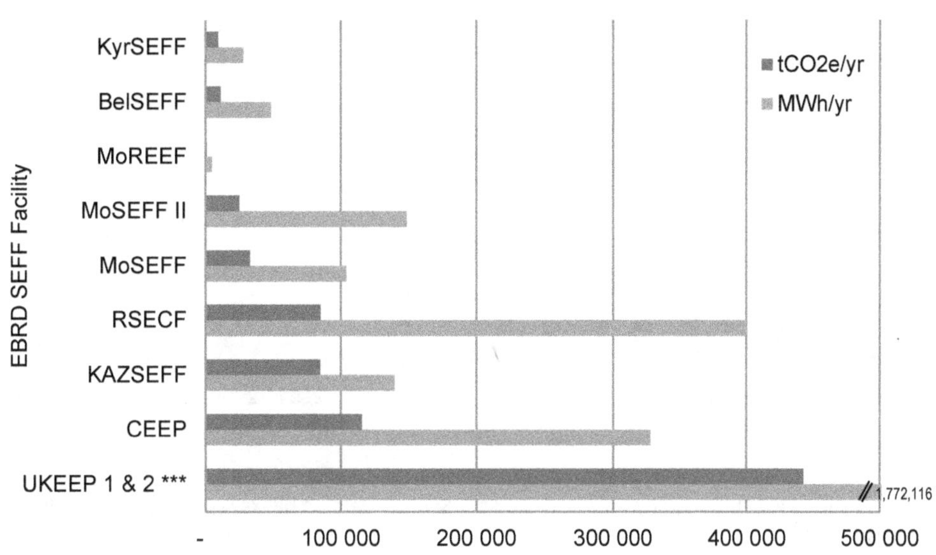

Source: Information provided by EBRD.

As of July 2012, IFC reports SME financial savings on energy costs under the Russia sustainable energy programme of USD 37 million per annum, equivalent to 1 805 GWh per annum. The GHG emission avoidance is 470 000 tCO_2e per annum[2].

Non-performing loan data

Some IFIs collect non-performing loan (NPL) data as part of the loan contract with the local financial institution. However, it is not routinely published by the IFIs. A recent EBRD study (Blyth and Savage, 2011) reported that while NPLs for corporates and SMEs in the Central and Eastern European region were relatively high following the financial crisis (up to 30% in some countries and 10% on average), the NPL ratio for the portfolio of SME loans financed under the SEFF was significantly lower than either the regional average or the equivalent EBRD SME loan portfolio outside of the SEFF. Similar effects have been reported for the IFC portfolio.

There are perhaps a number of reasons behind the lower default rate on sustainable energy type loans. These include the additional technical (e.g. energy audits) and financial (e.g. project cash flow and payback period analysis) due diligence process associated with preparing such loans for energy efficiency projects, allowing banks greater information with which to select companies. Financial incentives may also help credit performance (allowing banks to improve lending terms, or end users to meet payments through the provision of grants). Finally, those companies applying for energy efficiency finance may represent a self-selecting universe of higher quality borrowers, with a greater appreciation of their resource costs than others.

Figure 4.2. **Non-performing loan data for selected Central and Eastern European countries, 2010**

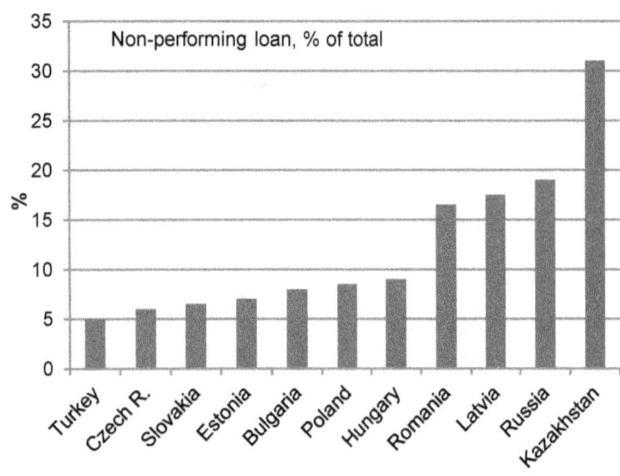

Source: Blyth and Savage (2011); Company data, UniCredit CEE Strategi Analysis, UniCredit Research.

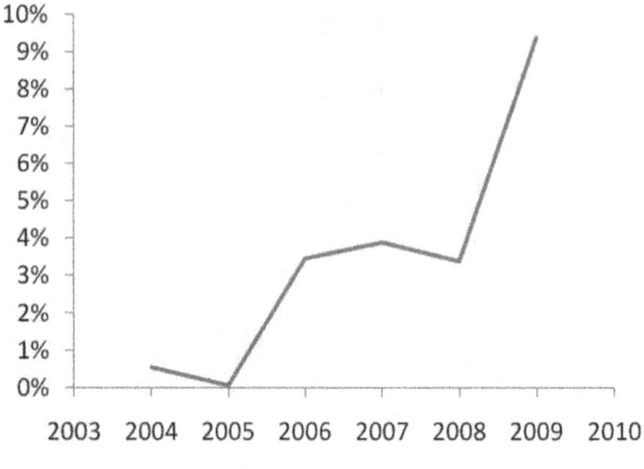

Source: Data on banks reporting NPLs in EBRD region from Amadeus https://amadeus.bvdinfo.com/version-20151023/home.serv?product=amadeusneo

Barriers and remedies

In the absence of public evaluation reports, information relating to the barriers faced during implementation of specific credit lines and what measures were undertaken to overcome them is not generally in the public domain, and can only be ascertained from more detailed research with the relevant IFI and FI staff. Several of the IFIs have undertaken evaluations of their environmental loan portfolio, but these are in restricted circulation. A high level overview of barriers drawn from the literature and general discussions with IFI representatives is presented in the next chapter.

Endnotes

1. See IFC Armenia Sustainable Energy Finance Program: www.ifc.org/wps/wcm/connect/REGION__EXT_Content/Regions/Europe+Middle+East+and+North+Africa/IFC+in+Europe+and+Central+Asia/Regional+Priorities/Climate+Change/Armenia+Sustainable+Energy+Finance+Project/

2. See IFC Russia Sustainable Energy Finance Program: www.ifc.org/wps/wcm/connect/RegProjects_Ext_Content/IFC_External_Corporate_Site/RSEFP_Home/Achievements/

References

Amadeus database: https://amadeus.bvdinfo.com/version-20151023/home.serv?product=amadeusneo

Blyth, W. and M. Savage (2011), *Financing Energy Efficiency: A Strategy for Reducing Lending Risk*, Chatham House Report. www.chathamhouse.org/sites/files/chathamhouse/19462_0511pp_blythsavage.pdf

EBRD (2013), *Introduction to EBRD's Sustainable Energy Initiative*. Presentation to the first Berlin climate finance workshop, 25th February 2013.

Zymelka, O., *Energy Efficiency Credit Lines, a Proposal by KfW*, presentation: www.energy-community.org/pls/portal/docs/174181.PDF

Chapter 5.

Barriers to environmental lending in EaP countries

Based on the analysis of the credit lines discussed earlier in the report and associated desk research, this chapter discusses the key barriers to environmental lending in the EU's Eastern Partnership (EaP) countries. These include both market and regulatory barriers, the nature of donor and International Finance Institutions (IFIs) support, and capacity issues faced by local financial institutions and their clients.

Environmental lending product life cycle

The promotion of environmentally-related (e.g. sustainable energy (SE) or energy efficiency (EE)) credit lines has been underway for nearly a decade in some EU's Eastern Partnership (EaP) and neighbouring markets. However, sustainable energy financing remains at an early stage of development. Few banks offer dedicated loan products or actively market the benefits of such investments. This is due to a number of potential market barriers. These can be categorised as regulatory (the enabling environment underpinning environmental lending), demand side (awareness and willingness among end borrowers to invest in environmental activities) and supply side (the capacity and willingness of local financial institutions (FIs) to develop products and the ability of International Finance Institutions (IFIs) to support them).

Before examining these barriers in more detail however we need to look at the product life cycle for an environmental product offered by banks. Knowing the life cycle of such products is important as it provides the basis for better understanding where some of the main barriers and challenges to increased environmental lending lie. We use the market development profile for sustainable energy product[1] as an example to frame this issue. Figure 5.1 illustrates the main stages of the sustainable energy finance life cycle.

Figure 5.1. **Major stages of sustainable energy finance product life cycle**

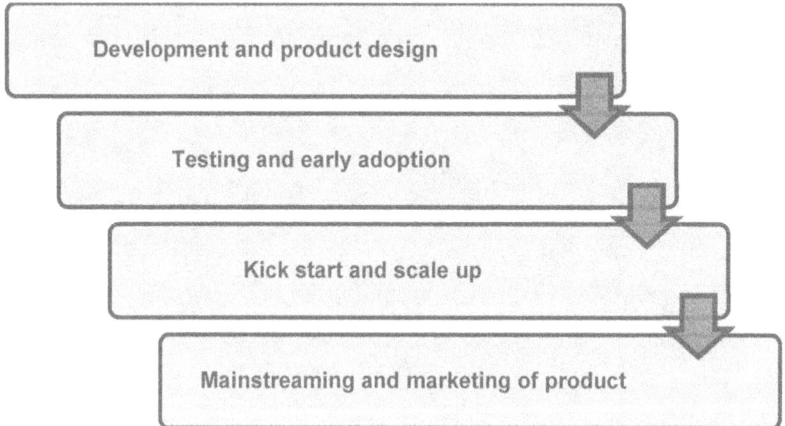

The first stage of the cycle is pre-launch or **development**. Typically, the cost of this stage is covered by the IFI and donor-funded technical cooperation (TC). Usually, this phase involves:

- Preparation of market demand studies – identifying market barriers and gaps, understanding market needs, identifying target groups and sustainable energy financing needs;
- Dialogue with relevant stakeholders: national authorities, international institutions, IFIs, professional and business associations, etc.;
- Assessment of policy and regulatory framework, sector and policy priorities;
- Determining the scope for improvement and indicative properties for sustainable energy products and operations;
- Assessing and understanding internal capabilities and resources of the financial institution;

- Determining additional support needs to reduce risks of failure in product launch (e.g., a dedicated TC package, building internal capacity, application of marketing techniques, etc.).

At the introduction stage the financial intermediaries may progress from **testing** of the product to **early adoption.** Typically, local FIs are cautious about deep involvement and large commitment to products they are not familiar with. They get involved at this stage with small size involvement, testing the market demand:

(i) *Testing* – financial intermediaries are increasingly hesitant when trying a new product and commit far fewer resources than necessary to become an early adopter. If this 'testing' experience is positive, they are likely to come back for more funding;

(ii) *Early Adoption* – at this stage financial intermediaries are usually involved in:

- Evaluation of the first results of the SE product launch;
- Design and launch of the first SE initiative, operations or products (rolling out the new tested financial product to further branches);
- Further SE product development and implementation of the new standards (technology standards, specific sector standards and tools, document and eligibility standards adapted to reflect actual market demand, new risk assessment and project appraisal procedures, etc.).

Once the SE product awareness is increased and the initial success achieved, the product gains momentum and experiences growth in sales. At this stage, financial institutions **kick-start** and further **upscale** SE operations:

(iii) *Kick-start* – this is when financial intermediaries:

- Having adopted the product and the internal procedures confidently identify and develop eligible projects;
- Continue assessing market demand for the innovative SE product and recognise positive market response in specific regional or client segments;
- Explore opportunities for up scaling SE operations;

(iv) *Scaling-up* – at this stage financial intermediaries gradually improve SE product or operations and focus on:

- Implementation of the feasible model; FIs extend their marketing and capacity building activities (these may involve class room trainings and "learning by doing" activities);
- Evaluation of the results and introduction of improved standards (e.g. focusing on the best performing projects, sector and sub-sector clusters, replicating best practices and techniques, etc.);
- Planning to and scaling-up SE operations to reach critical mass.

Finally, the financial institutions start to **mainstream** the product. As a result of successful mainstreaming of SE financing the ultimate **maturity** of the SE business operations is achieved:

(v) *Mainstreaming* – at this stage financial intermediaries:

- Include sustainable energy assessment in their loan assessment – for investment projects beyond those brought under specific energy efficiency programmes;
- Track SE investment opportunities (pipeline) and systematically report on SE investments implemented (portfolio);

vi) *Maturity* stage is characterised by:

- A critical mass of sustainable energy financing is achieved or partially achieved;
- The first signs of competition in the specific market segment are identified;
- Evaluation of the SE product or business area is performed covering the time from introduction to maturity and creating a base for the development of next product launch (respectively a new product or business operation will start the cycle from the first phase).

Figure 5.2 sets out the return on investment for an environmental lending product across its life cycle, based on EBRD experience.

Figure 5.2. **Return on investment across Sustainable Energy Finance life cycle**

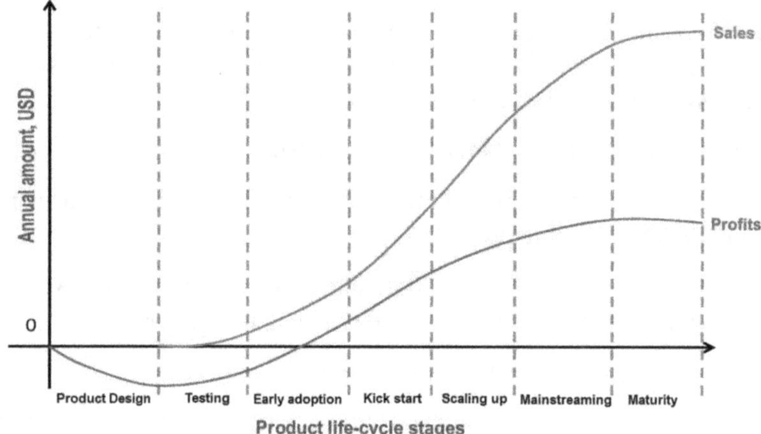

Source: EBRD (2014).

The implementation of an innovative lending product comes at high cost to FIs. They need to allocate resources and bring in efforts to launch and implement the product. Information systems, credit and risk assessment procedures, additional eligibility checks and document requirements, reporting, training, marketing, client and product differentiation are only a few examples of the processes that require adjustment to start sustainable energy lending. While FIs are offered long term funding and complementary technical assistance, many are not ready to take the burden of testing a sustainable energy product.

In this context, profitability for the FIs is negative particularly in the testing and in early adoption stages. As product sales grow steadily, the FIs carry a relatively high implementation and adaptation costs at the early stages of the product life cycle. Only towards the end of the early adaptation stage does the product become profitable for the FIs.

Using the knowledge accumulated while testing the product and early adoption of the product, some FIs may feel sufficiently confident to begin adopting environmental lending as a viable business product and may request further IFI help with a view to scaling up these operations by using their own financial resources. Some FIs choose to upscale operations through volume increase, others through testing and expanding into new sectors (e.g. from corporate to small and medium-sized enterprises (SME) or residential energy efficiency). As FIs achieve substantial scale of sustainable energy lending, they begin to mainstream operations to reduce the transaction costs for energy efficiency loans. Finally, product maturity and the peak of the product sales and market coverage is likely to be achieved if the FI adopts cross-selling into loan origination and includes sustainable energy investment potential in loan assessment processes for investment projects beyond those originated as a result of specific energy efficiency programmes. Mainstreaming is a significant undertaking and requires a financial services model that differs from that currently used by most traditional financial institutions.

Regulatory barriers

Regulatory barriers may prevent FIs from engaging in environmental lending, due to the lack of government support and strategic focus. A recent report on global climate finance identifies that the lack of a supportive enabling environment is often a bigger hurdle than the availability of finance (CPI, 2013). Environmental and climate change policy remains relatively weak in the EaP countries. There are a number of indices that have sought to measure the relative level of development of climate and sustainable energy policy in the region:

- The Climate Laws Institutions and Measures Index (CLIM), produced by EBRD, assesses countries across 4 key policy areas: international cooperation, domestic climate framework, sectoral fiscal or regulatory measures, and cross sectoral fiscal or regulatory measures;
- The Index of Sustainable Energy (ISE), produced by EBRD, measures countries on both their institutional arrangements as well as wider energy outcomes.

Table 5.1 sets out an assessment of the EaP countries.

Table 5.1. **Assessment of climate and sustainable energy policies and measures: EaP countries and Russia**

Country	CLIM Rating (Max=1)	ISE Rating: Institutions and incentives only (Max = 1)
Year	*2011*	*2008*
ARM	0.201	0.53
AZE	0.108	0.12
BLR	0.262	0.32
GEO	0.238	0.33
MDL	0.247	0.35
UKR	0.398	0.48
RUS	0.134	0.33

Source: EBRD (2011).

The EaP countries score relatively poorly against the indices for a number of reasons:

- *Low energy prices:* Energy prices are perhaps the biggest single factor in determining the level of investment that flows into energy efficiency products. Many markets continue to subsidise the costs of energy for reasons of either social protection or industrial competitiveness. This reduces the economic benefits from investing in energy efficiency, lowers the rates of return and increases the payback periods. Nonetheless, historic inefficiencies in industrial production and buildings design mean that significant economic potential remains even under subsidised pricing regimes.

- *Weak regulatory environment:* The policy environment remains weak in relation to encouraging borrowers to access environmental lending. Environmental benefits of clean technologies, such as reduction in greenhouse gas (GHG) emissions or pollutants, may not be recognised sufficiently in national legislation. This, in turn, distorts the economics of investment associated with environmental technologies. Uncertainty as to the future course of regulation can introduce uncertainty for private investors, particularly for investments with longer payback periods. Many countries do not have dedicated teams or institutions to support energy efficiency development.

Table 5.2 sets out a range of polices and measures that can support the development of a supportive environment for low-carbon development and environmental lending markets.

Table 5.2. **Overview of policies and measures to support low carbon development**

	Economic instruments	Regulatory instruments	Policy processes		
			Voluntary agreements	*Information*	*Technology R&D*
Improvement of energy efficiency	Energy taxes Lower energy subsidies Carbon taxes Fiscal incentives Tradable emissions permits	Minimum standards for power plants Best available techniques	Voluntary commitments to improving efficiency	Information and education campaigns	Funding to improve efficiency of cleaner fossil fuel generation
Switching to lower-carbon fuels	GHG permits Fiscal incentives Tradable emissions permits	Power plant fuel portfolio standards	Voluntary commitments to fuel switching	Information and education campaigns	Funding to improve efficiency of low-carbon generation technologies
Encouraging renewable alternatives	Capital grants Feed-in tariffs Quota obligations and permit trading GHG taxes Tradable emissions permits	Targets Supportive tariffs Grid access support	Voluntary commitments to install renewable capacity	Green electricity validation Information campaigns	Funding to improve efficiency of renewable generation technologies
Carbon sequestration	GHG taxes Tradable emissions permits	Emissions restrictions for major point emitters	Voluntary agreements to use carbon capture and storage	Information campaigns	

Source: Adapted from Metz et al (2007).

Demand side barriers

Strong demand for environmental finance is a key element in the creation of sustainable lending markets. As recent studies have concluded, weak demand may be a greater constraint than the lack of availability of environmental finance (Von Wolff and Phalpher, 2014, CPI, 2013). Many countries suffer from a lack of bankable green projects

(BMZ, 2014). Even with a strong regulatory and fiscal framework, challenges can be experienced in relation to both awareness of the benefits of environmental investment, and in relation to willingness to pay.

- *Lack of understanding of benefits among end borrowers:* Company managers take an overly conservative view when it comes to assessing energy savings potential. A survey of managers in the Russian Federation, undertaken by the International Finance Corporation (IFC), found that they consistently underestimated the technical potential and financial potential available. Due to a lack of cooperation between senior management and technical energy service personnel, promising projects that require considerable investment may be overlooked. Management teams are not always capable of correctly assessing the technical aspects or savings potential, while energy specialists often do not have a full understanding of a company's development and financing strategy. Energy is often not measured in a comprehensive way. Managers primarily turn their attention to a company's total energy expenses, rather than the share thereof in net costs, despite the fact that reducing the share of energy costs in total net production costs can improve profitability. As a result, even projects with high rates of return and short payback periods remain underfunded. Knowledge of environmental technologies and Best Available Techniques (BAT) may be limited in smaller companies or markets. Company managers tend to underestimate the importance of a systemic approach to energy efficiency, with little management attention or incentives provided.
- *Lack of willingness to borrow for energy efficiency:* Potentially high capital costs for energy efficiency equipment can act as a disincentive. Combined with a lack of willingness to borrow against uncertain future returns, particularly in more unstable markets, this can have a disincentive, even when returns are positive and payback periods short.

Table 5.3. **Key factors supporting end-borrower success**

Potential and Strategy	• Realistic estimate of energy efficiency potential • Development strategy will help determine energy demands • A step-by-step program: start with cost-efficient measures and gradually move to more capital intensive measures
Organisation	• Have a comprehensive strategy for energy efficiency • Appoint employees to supervise the project, award bonuses for project completion, get management involved, get technical and financial services involved • Keep detailed records of energy expenses at a departmental level or for the production divisions that have the highest levels of energy consumption
Financing	• Calculate the return on investment • Recognise the benefits of securing outside financing • Announce the situation on the financial market, including the availability of long term funds

Source: IFC (2006).

Supply side barriers

Some of the major barriers to the supply of environmental finance include:

- *Lack of familiarity:* Local financial institutions tend to lack familiarity with environmental lending products. These represent a departure from business as usual lending operations, and require an innovation mind set. A long period of IFI engagement is usually required to explain the functioning of such products.

- *Lack of FI capacity:* Environmental lending products through IFIs have strict technical performance standards. Such a product requires a significant investment in terms of staff time, information systems, credit and risk assessment procedures, eligibility checks, reporting procedures, and product marketing. While some of this is offset through the provision of external technical assistance during testing phase, for sustainable implementation, it must eventually be mainstreamed. Incentives also need to be aligned to encourage bank officers to engage.
- *Profitability and resource considerations:* A local financial institution implementing an innovative environmental lending product can experience high resource costs. The profitability may be negative in early testing and adoption phase as a result of the above demands.
- *IFI and donor support*: The scale and profile of donor support alongside a credit line may determine to what extent capacity issues identified above can be addressed. Poorly targeted support may prove a disincentive for further adoption, particularly where technical assistance is not properly mainstreamed into internal FI capacity.
- *Mismatch in project tenor:* Green projects (when not implemented for compliance reasons) are normally financed only if they can cover their own benefits (e.g. in terms of energy or resource savings). For many projects, this demands longer loan tenors due to the incremental costs of green technology. For many banks in the region this can create tenor mismatch between balance sheet assets and liabilities.

Endnotes

1. This development profile is taken from EBRD Success Note for its Sustainable Energy Finance Facility.

References

BMZ (2014), *Greening the Financial Sector – From Demonstration to Scale in Green Finance. Summary Highlights of the Symposium,* March 2014. KFW and BMZ. www.kfw-entwicklungsbank.de/PDF/Entwicklungsfinanzierung/Sektoren/Finanzsystementwicklung/Veranstaltungen/Symposium-Greening-the-Financial-Sector-summary-highlights.pdf

CPI (2013), *The Landscape of Climate Finance 2013* http://climatepolicyinitiative.org/wp-content/uploads/2013/10/The-Global-Landscape-of-Climate-Finance-2013.pdf

EBRD (2014), *Sustainable Energy Financing Facilities.* Internal discussion paper, EBRD, London.

EBRD (2011), *The Low Carbon Transition.* Report prepared in association with Grantham Research Institute on Climate Change and the Environment, EBRD, London. www.ebrd.com/news/publications/special-reports/special-report-on-climate-change-the-low-carbon-transition.html

IFC (2006), *On the Road to Energy Efficiency: Experience and Future Outlook. Researching Energy Efficiency Practices among Russian Companies*. Russia Sustainable Energy Finance Program, IFC, Washington DC. www.ifc.org/wps/wcm/connect/f35728804b5f68d48c39bd6eac26e1c2/Survey_English_text.pdf?MOD=AJPERES

Metz, B., Davidson, O. R., Bosch, P. R., & Meyer, L.A. (Eds.) (2007), *Climate Change 2007: Mitigation.* Contribution of Working Group III to the Fourth assessment report of the Intergovernmental Panel on Climate Change, Cambridge, UK, and New York, USA: Cambridge University Press. www.ipcc.ch/publications_and_data/publications_ipcc_fourth_assessment_report_wg3_report_mitigation_of_climate_change.htm

Wolff, S. von and K. Phalpher (2014), *Green Finance: Successes and Challenges – A Landscape Overview.* Prepared by Finance in Motion with contributions by Climate Policy Initiative, January 2014. www.kfw-entwicklungsbank.de/PDF/Entwicklungsfinanzierung/Sektoren/Finanzsystementwicklung/Veranstaltungen/2014_Symposium_Landscape-Study-Final-Version.pdf

Chapter 6.

Key drivers of sustainable environmental lending

Following the discussion on the barriers to environmental lending, this chapter sets out a framework for understanding how International Finance Institutions and donors might best approach the design and delivery of programmes for environmental lending, including both the design of credit lines and technical assistance for their implementation.

Key drivers for scaling up environmental lending

The ultimate goal of International Finance Institution (IFI) environmental lending products is to create a demand-driven self-sustaining market through local (commercially operated) financial institutions (FIs). Such markets may serve a steady financing demand from private and public sector entities, including households. The earlier analysis of the IFI portfolio identified a number of barriers to achieving such level of financing. On the basis of this analysis, we identify areas where donor and IFI support may be important to ensure the scale up of environmental lending. These areas, or key drivers, can be grouped around 3 key factors:

- *FI engagement:* the ability to persuade FIs to adopt environmental lending practices;
- *Product delivery:* the capacity to design and disburse credit lines in an effective manner;
- *Market sustainability:* the extent to which policy/market drivers support ongoing lending.

Each of these drivers, with their specific motivations, are discussed in more detail further below.

Figure 6.1. **Key drivers to develop and scale up environmental lending**

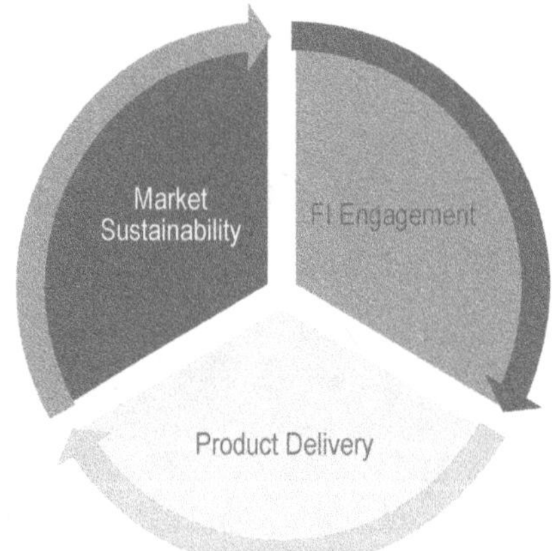

FI Engagement	Product Delivery	Market Sustainability
▪ Access to finance ▪ Concessionality ▪ Technical advisory ▪ Market positioning ▪ Business development ▪ Minimal resource demand	▪ Resources and staffing ▪ Skills and capacity building ▪ Product design and promotion ▪ Effective pipeline development ▪ Adoption of tools and methods ▪ Robust appraisal and reporting	▪ Strong investment climate ▪ Environmental policy support ▪ Access to finance ▪ Effective donor support

FI Engagement

The first set of key success factors relate to the capacity of IFIs to engage with and persuade local FIs to accept funding for and develop environmental lending products. Environmental finance remains a product that needs to be sold to FIs, rather than one for which there is a strong natural demand. There are a number of challenges and barriers in this regard. Local FIs are often unfamiliar with the definitions, eligibility and reporting frameworks used by the IFIs for environmental credit lines. Environmental lending may be perceived as more complex to appraise, more difficult to promote to customers, and more onerous in terms of reporting.

We recognise the following potential motivations for local FIs to engage with IFI environmental credit lines:

- *Building profitable market share:* A small number of FIs may consider that environmental lending provides a significant growth opportunity. Against a backdrop of rising energy prices, tighter environmental legislation and more robust efficiency standards, FIs may identify environmental lending as a potentially profitable market. By early positioning, they hope to achieve first mover advantage and take a dominant share. The promotion by IFIs of environmental finance draws heavily upon this narrative, even if in early testing and adoption phases, the product is likely to require net investment by the FI.
- *Addressing liquidity issues*: Many of the EU's Eastern Partnership (EaP) countries have been experiencing tight credit conditions since 2008 associated with the problems in global financial markets. For a small number of FIs, the provision of funds for environmental purposes has become an attractive route to addressing liquidity requirements, particularly where these funds address existing customer segments, and where the IFI has already lent on more mainstream products (e.g. small and medium sized enterprises (SME) and is now seeking to push additionality. The local FI pipeline may already contain eligible projects that would have otherwise been financed through more mainstream products (SME, residential loans), and the additional costs of origination are therefore not significant. It should be noted that this represents a small percentage, as most FIs tend to have a wider relationship with IFIs, and an environmental lending product does not normally represent the first lending relationship between the institutions.
- *Credit line concessionality and tenor*: Generally, IFIs are committed to not distorting commercial lending markets unless there is a clear market failure and associated development benefit. The cost of IFI funds is often not the lowest available to commercial banks, although tenor is often longer than that available elsewhere. IFI credit lines are also perceived to have more robust conditionality and reporting criteria. However, interest rates offered on IFI environmental credit lines may be more concessional than for other products (such as SME credit lines), making them more attractive for local FIs. This reflects the potential development impact, and the public good associated with addressing environmental externalities. Lower rates may be achieved through the blending with donor grant finance, or by IFI board approval based on the expected demonstration effect. FIs may accept an environmental lending component alongside a more mainstream credit product in order to improve the terms on which it is offered.

- *The provision of grant-based technical assistance*: IFI credit lines are often accompanied by substantial technical assistance. This support can range from pipeline development, staff training, project preparation, project appraisal, technical implementation and monitoring and verification. Such activities are often grant-supported, and provided to FIs and their clients free, or on heavily subsidised terms. This can be a powerful driver of FI participation (as well as for customer take up), both from a capacity building perspective, as well as by reducing the resource burden of product development and compliance.
- *Environmental positioning:* Some FIs have developed social and environmental policies, and seek to position themselves as proactive in addressing climate change, or resource issues. This may be particularly true for those with significant international representation amongst their shareholder base. Engaging on dedicated environmental lending products can demonstrate a level of commitment to the banks ethical or environmental involvement. Such activities can form the basis of corporate social responsibility (CSR) reporting and be used for media and marketing purposes. In addition, IFI clients may be required to adopt or meet higher environmental or social performance standards than would be expected under national laws. International Finance Corporation (IFC) cascades its performance standards to its clients. Of the eight standards, two relate directly to environmental performance (see Table 6.1).
- *Establishing credibility:* The prospect of partnership with an IFI can be attractive for the management team of a local FI. Such a partnership can build market credibility and positioning. In transition economies, there is a perception that IFI due diligence procedures are robust and a willingness to partner provide an indicator of corporate health. Partner banks may promote the IFI partnership prominently on their website and other corporate communication materials.

Table 6.1. **IFC Performance standards**

Performance Standard	Objectives
PERFORMANCE STANDARD (PS) 1: **Assessment and management of environmental and social risks and impacts**	▪ Identify project environmental and social risks and impacts ▪ Adopt mitigation hierarchy ▪ Anticipate, avoid ▪ Minimize ▪ Compensate or offset ▪ Improve performance through an Environmental and Social Management System (ESMS) ▪ Engagement with Affected Communities, other stakeholders ▪ Throughout project cycle, include communications, grievance mechanisms
PERFORMANCE STANDARD (PS) 3: **Resource efficiency and pollution prevention**	▪ Avoid, minimize, and reduce project related pollution ▪ More sustainable use of resources, including energy and water ▪ Reduced project related greenhouse gas (GHG) emissions

Source: IFC (2012).

Product delivery

The second set of key drivers relates to the ability of local FIs to successfully design a product that will allow them to disburse IFI credit lines. Where the credit line disbursement proves problematic or overly resource intensive, it is unlikely that there will be a product continuation. Barriers include a limited project pipeline, lack of customer awareness, inadequate staffing and skills, inadequate incentives, and a lack of commitment from senior management. We identify the following key success factors in effective design and disbursement:

- *Product design and promotion:* Local FIs need to design products that are financially attractive and with a strong narrative. The financing model should be based on the local context and the marketing needs of the bank's clients. The product should be focused initially on core business segments before moving on to new markets. It is important that any IFI concessionality is passed through to end borrowers. FIs should also recognise that their customer base may not be primarily motivated by environmental concerns, and that environmental benefits (such as greenhouse gas (GHG) emission mitigation), may be secondary to the financial benefits associated with increased productivity or reduced energy bills.
- *Integration with institutional strategies:* Environmental lending works most effectively where it maps onto existing operational structures and processes. Sustainable energy products need to be properly integrated into the banks' institutional procedures, but nonetheless separated from the core business activities. Local financial institutions might consider deploying a matrix structure (with dual reporting lines) where an energy efficiency product is managed separately, but as a subset of SME or residential lending. However, this is particularly challenging, with local FIs often not seeing the benefits of such a complex management structure.
- *Resources and staffing:* While it is important that environmental lending should map as much as possible onto existing FI structures and processes, a lack of investment in staffing may indicate a low level of commitment to the project. Ideally, environmental lending products are supported not only by a dedicated product manager or team at headquarters (depending on the size of the credit line and the complexity of the product), but also by responsible/informed lending officers in regional branches. However, this may only be commercially viable where demand is sufficiently high, and where the value of transactions is sufficiently large. There should be a recognition that such products require a level of upfront investment in staff and procedures, even if they take advantage of existing resources.
- *Skills and capacity building:* Environmental lending products are potentially more complex in their appraisal and reporting. Staff will often require training to recognise potential customer opportunities, communicate benefits to customers, ensure that loan applications meet eligibility criteria, and to report on key indicators. Support is often provided by donor-funded technical assistance grant facilities that allow FIs to mitigate technical risks through the use of external consultants or by the creation of in-house specialist teams (e.g. EBRD – Ukreximbank). Over time, these skills can be mainstreamed into the organisation.
- *Internal messaging and incentives:* Clear internal messaging from senior management about the importance of the environmental lending product is required. The alignment of staff incentives is also important. Without these, there

may be a perception that the product is a "one off" and its promotion by loan officers will remain of secondary importance to other products perceived as more strategically important or lucrative.

- *Effective pipeline development:* A strong project pipeline is important to the success of a dedicated credit line. At the SME and household level, a significant proportion of the existing customer base may be eligible for targeted environmental products without significant additional support – staff simply need to be able to recognise eligible activities. For more complex corporate lending projects, local FIs may choose to co-develop eligible and bankable projects with their client base, potentially with the support of IFI-funded external consultants.
- *Adoption of tools and methods:* Products that measure energy savings or GHG emission mitigation benefits will require some level of technical calculation derived from equipment performance and standards. Such calculations are ordinarily performed by qualified engineers. FIs may adopt specific tools (e.g. energy saving calculators, CO_2 calculators) to support their staff in the appraisal of projects. IFIs and their consultants may develop standard web-based tools to allow bank staff to assess and appraise economic and environmental aspects of their portfolio for reporting purposes.
- *Robust appraisal and reporting:* Environmental credit lines carry with them enhanced reporting and verification requirements associated with the externality being addressed. This requires more robust *ex-ante* technical appraisal processes (*i.e.* to assess whether a project might be expected to deliver adequate energy and other resource savings) and *ex-post* verification (to measure these savings and to report on the associated environmental benefits – e.g. CO_2 abatement). Such activities can be resource intensive, particularly for smaller clients and loan values, and often require significant IFI/donor support to deliver.

Market sustainability

The third set of key success factors relate to the market and policy environment in which the environmental lending product is to be developed. While IFIs may successfully engage with a local FI and assist in the successful disbursement of the credit line, without a supportive market environment, FIs are unlikely to commit to supporting ongoing lending operations without continuing IFI support. This can be particularly true where the IFI has provided significant support in terms of concessionality and/or technical assistance to support disbursement. Without the demonstration effect of a local FI building a sustainable lending product, other local financial institutions are less likely to enter the market.

A number of market and policy barriers have been identified earlier in the report. These include poor private sector investment climate, lack of supportive and consistent policy frameworks for environmental investment, and limited access to finance beyond IFI sources. Some of the key factors that can help reduce the above barriers include:

- *Strong investment climate:* Sustainable environmental lending requires a supportive investment climate (strong investor protection, governance, competition policy and regulation). While common to other sectors, such factors nonetheless are a pre-requisite for investment in relevant sectors such as renewables, waste and energy efficiency. Private sector investors are unlikely to invest in environmental outcomes where there is a level of political and regulatory risk.

- *Environmental policy support:* Customers must be sufficiently mandated or incentivised to engage with environmental lending products. A supportive policy environment may include legislation mandating environmental standards (e.g. buildings efficiency standards, industrial equipment, Best Available Techniques (BAT), incentives promoting certain types of renewable energy sources (obligations or feed-in tariffs), or the removal of market distorting subsidies (e.g. fossil fuel support) that reduce incentives for investment in clean alternatives or their efficient use. Goals may be supported by the use of trading systems and/or taxation (e.g. emissions trading), and incentives (e.g. tax rebates, accelerated depreciation). Policy goals need to be both coherent (linking permitting and licensing to economic instruments) and long term (e.g. targets and pathways).
- *Access to finance:* A sustainable environmental lending market is only possible if FI access to finance can be sustained without ongoing concessional support. This requires developed domestic debt markets, and accessible rates and tenor of loans for potential customer segments. It also depends on the extent to which specific stakeholder groups (corporates, SMEs, households) can access domestic finance to achieve environmental objectives, either through mainstream lending (e.g. SME loans) or using specific lending products (e.g. energy efficiency loans), potentially supported by risk mitigation instruments or other donor funds.
- *Network support:* Banks operating in a network of other financial institutions supporting similar products (such as through the Sustainable Energy Finance Facilities model used by EBRD), can benefit from shared insights, pooled technical resources and other network benefits. Challenges remain, however, in relation to capacity transfer due to issues of competition and intellectual property rights protection.
- *Phased product development:* FIs need first to leverage on their core operations to deliver value added sustainable energy financing and advisory to their existing clients; and second to acquire appropriate marketing and management capacities before they diversify activities and divert scarce resources into new business areas (e.g. for an SME bank moving into residential energy efficiency sector, etc.).
- *Effective donor support:* Given limited capital, local FIs are most likely to pursue market segments where the resource requirements and complexity are low, product returns high and the market large. This represents a potential opportunity cost for developing environmental lending products (for example, the commercial market for such products remains limited in OECD countries). A key challenge is the resource demand associated with pipeline development and the preparation of bankable projects. Donors have therefore sought to address this through the provision of extensive technical assistance support (often free and outsourced). While underpinning FI engagement and credit line disbursement, the over-provision of technical support and concessional funds may both intensify FI perceptions of product complexity and slow the transfer of skills and capacity to the local market. Both of these can undermine longer term market development. The result is that FIs may choose to pursue such products with the same levels of concessional finance and technical assistance. Likewise, IFIs may become accustomed to providing follow-on credit lines to existing borrowers in order to meet internal lending targets. Going forward, IFIs may have to broaden their role towards de-risking the flow of third party public and private finance, rather than to meeting their own lending targets (BMZ, 2014).

References

BMZ (2014), *Greening the Financial Sector – From Demonstration to Scale in Green Finance. Summary Highlights of the Symposium,* March 2014. KFW and BMZ. www.kfw-entwicklungsbank.de/PDF/Entwicklungsfinanzierung/Sektoren/Finanzsystementwicklung/Veranstaltungen/Symposium-Greening-the-Financial-Sector-summary-highlights.pdf

IFC (2012), Performance Standards on Environmental and Social Sustainability, IFC, World Bank Group, www.ifc.org/wps/wcm/connect/c8f524004a73daeca09afdf998895a12/IFC_Performance_Standards.pdf?MOD=AJPERES

Annex A.

Questionnaire for stakeholder consultations

Objectives of the Questionnaire

The main objective of this Questionnaire is to support consultations with a range of stakeholders involved in shaping environmental lending policies in the respective review country. We hope that such consultations will help the Project Team better understand the challenges to and opportunities for increased lending to green investments in the EU's Eastern Partnership countries. With this in mind, the Questionnaire has been designed to serve as an interview guide for the Project Team's consultations with key groups of stakeholders (for types of stakeholders, see Figure 1.3).

Structure of the Questionnaire

The Questionnaire consists of two main parts: (i) Factual data table; and (ii) Semi-structured questionnaire. Through the Factual data table, the Project Team will aim to collect quantitative information from the participating local Financing Institution (FI) and the partner International Finance Institution (IFI). However, where appropriate, other data sources will be used.

The Semi-structured questionnaire is organised around four thematic sections which include: (i) IFI engagement with IFs; (ii) financial product design and delivery; (iii) monitoring, reporting and verification; and, (iv) sustainability of products offered through the credit line. The financial product design and delivery section has a number of sub-sections addressing particular aspects of credit line design and implementation as well as the IF capacity to manage such financial products and the response of the market to the specific green products offered by the local FI. As indicated in the Questionnaire, each question may be relevant to more than one stakeholder.

Method of work

The Questionnaire will be sent to the institutions which will be interviewed, in advance of the meetings with the Project Team. The issues covered in the Questionnaire are in no way exhaustive and should not be seen as limiting the discussion. The Questionnaire will be further tailored to the specific country and bank which will participate in the study. In preparation for the discussions with the Project Team, interviewees will be referred to the section which is relevant to their institution.

Table A.1. **Factual data table**

Criteria	Data inputs
Maturity of local banking sector	
Getting credit index	World Bank Doing business report
Financial market development index	World Economic Forum Global Competitiveness Report
Domestic credit provided by the banking sector as a share of GDP	EBRD Structural change indicators (Banking sector depth and financial sector development)
Domestic credit to households (% of GDP)	EBRD/Others
Ratio of bank capital to assets	EBRD/Others (Bank solvency and resiliency)
Ratio of bank non-performing loans to total gross loans	EBRD/Others (Credit portfolio quality and efficiency)
Interest rate spread	World Bank Development Indicators database/Others (Financial sector efficiency in intermediation)
Risk premium on lending	World Bank Development Indicators database (Perceived private sector risk premium)
Asset share of foreign-owned banks and state-owned banks	EBRD/Others (Level of international/private sector participation)
Maturity of environmental regulation	
Energy intensity	MWh/$ GDP (benchmarked)
Carbon intensity	tCO_2e/$ GDP (benchmarked)
Energy pricing	Energy prices (benchmarked) Overview of renewable energy and fossil fuel subsidies (by segment)
Energy efficiency regulation	Minimum standards (buildings, industrial equipment, fuel efficiency) Demand side management, awareness programmes
Energy (resource) efficiency incentives	Tax and other fiscal incentives (e.g. accelerated depreciation, reduced custom duties, tax credits)
Other support	Other relevant environmental or resource efficiency legislation
Profile of borrowing Financial Institution	
Type of institution	E.g. Bank, leasing company
Share capital	Called up share capital Main shareholders, % of international shareholders
Main product segments	Product lines and key market segments % share of revenue by product
No employees	#
No of branches	#
Geographical coverage	Regions of operation
Social and environmental policies	E.g. international environmental and social standards, Climate change strategy
Environmental products	E.g. energy efficiency loans, resource efficiency, water, renewable energy
Previous engagement with IFIs	Overview of previous engagement with IFIs

Criteria	Data inputs
IFI credit line profile	
Purpose of IFI credit line	General description of credit line
Eligibility criteria	Copy of eligibility criteria applied to FI
Duration of IFI credit line	Years
Total value of IFI credit line	$ mln
Other debt leveraged (domestic)	$ mln, origin of funds
Other debt leveraged (international)	$ mln, origin of funds
Donor or other public funds associated	$ mln, origin of funds, use of funds
Ex-ante indicators	Performance and reporting indicators associated with the credit line
FI loan product profile	
Customer profile(s)	(e.g. MSME, SME, corporate, residential, housing, municipal, other)
Project profile	Profile of projects, eligibility criteria (if additional to IFI)
Number of sub-borrowers	#
Approval rate	% of applications approved
Typical turnover of sub-borrowers (where applicable)	$ mln
Project profile	Data on use of funds (split by industry or type or technology)
Loan value	$ mln, (range and average value)
Repayment period	Years, (range and average value)
Interest rate	%, (range and average value)
Collateral requirements	Typical % of loan value, description
Variation of terms with products for similar customer segments	Description of variation
Credit line performance and impact	
Time to fully disburse credit line	Years
Default rate	% of non-performing loans
Default rate on comparable segment	% of non-performing loans
Environmental impact indicators	tCO_2e avoided MWh saved, MW installed, other resource savings
Ex-post monitoring	Description of reporting and impact assessment *ex-post*
Product line continuation post disbursement	Yes/No

Table A.2. **Semi-structured questionnaire**

Question?	IFI	IFI Consultant	FI Senior	FI Officer	Borrower	Policy maker	Other
International finance institution (IFI) engagement with local Financial institutions (FIs)							
What were the strategic drivers for the FI to invest in developing an environmental loan product?	X		X				
How did the development of an environmental lending product fit into a broader corporate strategy?	X		X				
Did the FI board or shareholders suggest or support the development of an environmental product?	X		X				
Is there significant international FI shareholding, and has this influenced product development?	X		X				
Did the FI offer other environmental or resource oriented products prior to this credit line?	X		X				
Did the FI have a clear social and environmental policy, and did this influence product development?	X		X				
How important was the issue of liquidity and access to funds in agreeing the loan?	X		X				
Was there a level of concessionality attached to the funds? How important was this?	X		X				
Has the IFI raised the capital to support the credit line at a concessional rate?	X						
Were there other grant funds deployed alongside the credit line? How important was this?							
Were regulatory or market trends important for the FI in deciding to implement the product?	X		X				
Was the credit line supported by technical assistance? On what terms, and how important was this?	X		X				
Were there additional debt or grant facilities received from other sources to support the credit line?	X		X				

Question?	IFI	IFI Consultant	FI Senior	FI Officer	Borrower	Policy maker	Other
FI product design and delivery							
Design							
How did the FI product differ from other credit products offered by the FI?	X	X	X	X			
What were the innovative design features, if any?	X	X	X	X			
How did the commercial terms (interest rate, tenor, collateral) differ from similar segment products?	X	X	X	X			
Were cash flow/project finance assessments used to assess affordability?	X	X	X	X			
What end use eligibility criteria were developed and how were they applied?	X	X	X	X			
What other support was provided to potential borrowers and why?	X	X	X	X			
How did reporting requirements for end borrowers differ from other FI products?	X	X	X	X			
FI capacity							
What additional level of resourcing was required to service the product (staff, other resources?)	X	X	X	X			
How many staff were responsible for delivering the product? How were they chosen?	X	X	X				
Did FI staff have the technical capacity to understand the product?	X	X	X	X			
Did FI staff have the technical capacity to appraise loan applications?	X	X	X	X			
What training was provided to FI staff to support product promotion and application analysis?							
Were any new tools or methodologies adopted by the FI to support the product?	X	X	X	X			
What were the challenges in marketing the product to borrowers and how were these overcome?	X	X	X	X			
What were the incremental marketing costs and how were they covered?		X	X				
What level of technical assistance or outsourcing (pipeline, appraisal, checking) was used to support delivery?	X	X	X	X			
Market response and access							
How quickly was the credit line disbursed compared to other products in the same segment?	X		X	X			
What were the most attractive features of the product for end borrowers?	X		X	X	X		
What was the main motivation of the end borrower to take on a loan?		X	X	X	X		
Were there any similar products being offered by other FIs, and how did they differ?	X		X	X	X		

Question?	IFI	IFI Consultant	FI Senior	FI Officer	Borrower	Policy maker	Other
Was other concessional/grant finance available to borrowers and did this impact credit line success?	X		X				
FI product design and delivery - continued							
Market response and access - continued							
What other options were considered by end borrowers to finance their projects?				X	X		
Did potential borrowers find the product easy to understand and the potential benefits clear?				X	X		
How was the product promoted? Were climate and environmental benefits clearly explained?				X	X		
Were the application procedures simple compared to other products targeting similar segments?				X	X		
What were the end user reporting requirements? Were these an issue in agreeing loans?				X	X		
How important was the offer of project or technical support to end borrowers (if any)?				X	X		
What other barriers or concerns were identified by borrowers when considering the product?				X	X		
Did the profile of end borrowers differ from borrowers in similar segments and how?				X	X		
Were end borrower decisions influenced by policy or regulation (e.g. efficiency standards, incentives)?				X	X	X	X
What changes would have made it more likely to take the loan product?					X		
Is it likely that you will take a similar product again?					X		
Project implementation							
Were there issues in identifying suitable equipment to meet eligibility criteria?		X		X	X		
Were there issues in procuring the equipment or technology at a reasonable price?		X		X	X		
Were there issues of installation or integration of the equipment?		X		X	X		
Has the equipment performed according to expectations since installation?		X		X	X		
How important was technical assistance provided through the FI during implementation?		X		X	X		
Monitoring, reporting and verification							
What indicators were used to track performance and delivery of the loan?		X		X	X		
How was project implementation monitored and verified?		X		X	X		
Were the reporting requirements easy to comply with?		X		X	X		

Question?	IFI	IFI Consultant	FI Senior	FI Officer	Borrower	Policy maker	Other
Sustainability							
Was the loan product profitable for the FI, taking into account all resource requirements?			X				
How did the costs of developing and managing the product compare to those in similar segments?			X				
How does the default rate on the FI portfolio differ from that of other product lines? Why?			X				
Have there been any opportunity costs for the FI associated with developing the product?			X				
Has there been a continuation of the product after full disbursement of the IFI credit line?	X		X				
…If yes, have ongoing operations received further concessional funds or grant support?	X		X				
…If yes, have the new operations maintained the same eligibility criteria as the IFI credit line?			X				
…If not, what are the main reasons for discontinuation?	X		X				
Have there been other market entrants offering similar products since the product was marketed?	X		X		X		
Have the impact and benefits of the product been shared with policy makers and other stakeholders?	X		X			X	X
What expected changes in regulation will increase demand for such products? How?	X		X		X	X	X
What expected changes in markets and resource prices will increase demand for such products?	X		X		X	X	X
What are the key barriers to developing legislation promoting environmental and sustainable measures?	X					X	X
To what extent do developments in EU environmental and climate policy influence the local market?	X					X	X
What would be the key policy and regulatory developments that would support demand?	X		X			X	X
How can concessional funds best be used to ensure the sustainability of products in the market?	X		X			X	X

Annex B.

Policy and market analysis

A market overview will be undertaken in the relevant country, drawing upon the frameworks presented in recent OECD papers "Policy guidance for investment in clean energy infrastructure" and "Towards a green investment policy framework: The case of low-carbon, climate-resilient infrastructure". The analysis framework will be tailored to the market and sector identified for the credit line case studies once selected. The aim will be to identify the specific market, regulatory and investment challenges associated with scaling up environmental lending in the given sector, and to explore how governments might support this process going forward. The following broad topics will be covered through a combination of desk research and discussions with policy makers:

- *Investment climate:* To what extent the underlying drivers enabling private sector investment are present, including investor protection, intellectual property rights and technology development, contract enforcement, public governance, and fair competition policy in relation to state-owned enterprises;
- *Policy support:* To what extent are environmental objectives reflected in policy frameworks, including the pricing of externalities (e.g. CO_2 emissions), removal of fossil fuel subsidies, long term targets (e.g. in relation to energy efficiency, renewable energy, greenhouse gas (GHG) emission reductions), coherent policy goals, the use of investment incentives and other fiscal instruments, and streamlined permitting and licensing;
- *Access to finance:* To what extent specific stakeholder groups (corporates, small and medium-sized enterprises (SMEs), households) can access domestic finance to achieve environmental objectives, either through mainstream lending (e.g. SME loans) or using specific lending products (e.g. energy efficiency loans), potentially supported by risk mitigation instruments or other donor funds.

Glossary

Accelerated depreciation	Any method of depreciation used for accounting or income tax purposes that allows greater deductions in the earlier years of the life of an asset. For tax purposes, accelerated depreciation provides a way of deferring corporate income taxes by reducing taxable income in current years, in exchange for increased taxable income in future years. This is a valuable tax incentive that encourages businesses to purchase new assets.
Additionality	Additionality is a notional measurement of an intervention (i.e., doing something), when the intervention is compared to a baseline, *status quo* metric (i.e., doing nothing). The 'intervention' can be based on either technology or economics.
Asset price bubble	An asset price bubble is characterised by a surge in prices of asset (e.g. housing, stock or gold) that raises expectations of further increases that generate a succession of increases until confidence falters, the bubble "bursts", and prices rapidly revert to an objectively-based level.
Best available techniques	Best Available Techniques (BAT) are defined in Article 2(11) of EU Directive 96/61/EC on Integrated Pollution Prevention and Control (IPPC) as "the most effective and advanced stage in the development of activities and their methods of operation which indicate the practical suitability of particular techniques for providing, in principle, the basis for emission limit values designed to prevent and, where that is not practicable, generally to reduce emissions and the impact on the environment as a whole." Article 2(11) clarifies that "techniques" includes both the technology used and the way in which the installation is designed, built, maintained, operated and decommissioned.
Carbon capture and storage	Carbon capture and storage (CCS) is the process of capturing waste CO_2 from large point sources, such as fossil fuel power plants, transporting it to a storage site, and depositing it where it will not enter the atmosphere, normally an underground geological formation. The aim is to prevent the release of large quantities of CO_2 into the atmosphere.
Carbon intensity	The amount of emissions of CO_2 per unit of GDP.
Carbon sequestration	The process of carbon capture and storage, where CO_2 is removed from flue gases, such as on power stations, before being stored in underground reservoirs. Similar to CCS.
Carbon tax	A carbon tax is a levy on the carbon content of fossil fuels. Because virtually all of the carbon in fossil fuels is ultimately emitted as CO_2 when burning fuels, a carbon tax is equivalent to an emission tax on each unit (tonne) of CO_2-equivalent emissions. A carbon tax puts a price on each tonne of GHG emitted, sending a price signal that will, over time, elicit a market response across the entire economy, resulting in reduced emissions. It has the advantage of providing an incentive without favouring any one way of reducing emissions over another. By reducing fuel consumption, increasing fuel efficiency, using cleaner fuels and adopting new technology, businesses and individuals can reduce the amount they pay in carbon tax, or even offset it altogether.

Collateral	Property or other assets that a borrower offers a lender to secure a loan. If the borrower stops making the promised loan payments, the lender can seize the collateral to recoup its losses. Because collateral offers some security to the lender in case the borrower fails to pay back the loan, loans that are secured by collateral typically have lower interest rates than unsecured loans.
Concentration ratio	Concentration Ratio represents the percentage of total industry output which a given number of large firms account for. The five-bank concentration ratio (CR5) measures the relative weight of the first five banks on the overall banking system from the point of view of bank assets.
Concessionality	The degree of concessionality of a loan is measured by its "grant element". The grant element is defined as the difference between the loan's nominal value (face value) and the sum of the discounted future debt-service payments to be made by the borrower (present value), expressed as a percentage of the loan's face value. Whenever the interest rate charged for a loan is lower than the discount rate, the present value of the debt is smaller than its face value, with the difference reflecting the (positive) grant element of the loan (World Bank definition).
Cost of capital	The cost of capital is the rate of return that capital could be expected to earn in an alternative investment of equivalent risk.
Debt overhang	A debt burden that is so large that an entity cannot take on additional debt to finance future projects, even those that are profitable enough to enable it to reduce its indebtedness over time.
Deleveraging	The process by which financial institutions and investors reduce the relative size of their assets to equity ratio. Generally, it means shedding assets in the financial sector, thus reducing credit and slowing the economy.
Discounting	A mathematical operation making monetary (or other) amounts received or expended at different points in time (years) comparable across time. The operator uses a fixed or possibly time-varying discount rate (>0) from year to year that makes future value worth less today. In a descriptive discounting approach one accepts the discount rates people (savers and investors) actually apply in their day-to-day decisions (private discount rate). In a prescriptive (ethical or normative) discounting approach the discount rate is fixed from a social perspective, e.g. based on an ethical judgment about the interests of future generations (social discount rate).
Due diligence	The responsibility of bank directors and managers to act in a prudent manner in evaluating credit applications.
Energy intensity	The ratio of energy use to economic output. At the national level, energy intensity is the ratio of total domestic primary energy use or final energy use to Gross Domestic Product.
ESCO	An Energy service company (ESCO) that offers a broad range of energy services to end-users, including the design and implementation of energy savings projects, retrofitting, energy conservation, energy infrastructure outsourcing, power generation, energy supply, and risk management. ESCO guarantees the energy savings to be achieved tying them directly to its remuneration, as well as finances or assists in acquiring financing for the operation of the energy system, and retains an on-going role in monitoring the savings over the financing term.

Feed-in tariff	The price per unit of electricity that a utility or power supplier has to pay for distributed or renewable electricity fed into the grid by non-utility generators. A public authority regulates the tariff. Feed-in tariff is a policy mechanism designed to accelerate investment in renewable energy technologies by offering long-term contracts to renewable energy producers, typically based on the cost of generation of each technology. Feed-in tariffs often include "tariff digression", a mechanism by which the price (or tariff) ratchets down over time in order to track and encourage technological cost reductions. The goal of feed-in tariffs is to offer cost-based compensation to renewable energy producers, thus providing the price certainty and long-term contracts that help finance renewable energy investments.
Fixed interest rate	Fixed interest rate refers to any type of debt instrument, such as a loan, bond, mortgage, or credit, that does not fluctuate during the life of the instrument.
Grace period	A provision in most loan and insurance contracts which allows payment to be received for a certain period of time after the actual due date. During this period no late fees will be charged, and the late payment will not result in default or cancellation of the loan.
Hedge	A risk management strategy used in limiting or offsetting the probability of loss from fluctuations in the prices of commodities, currencies, or securities.
Interest	Interest is a fee paid by a borrower of assets to the owner as a form of compensation for the use of the assets. It is most commonly the price paid for the use of borrowed money, or money earned by deposited funds.
Leverage (ratio)	The leverage ratio is the proportion of debts that a bank has compared to its equity / capital. A bank's leverage ratio gives the proportion of its assets funded by equity capital (which absorbs losses) rather than debt or deposits (which do not). When a bank's balance sheet is financed with more of its equity capital, it is better able to absorb losses on its assets. So a bank is less vulnerable to a rise in defaults on its loans or a market downturn that depresses the prices of assets it holds. When regulators impose a higher leverage ratio, the goal is to make banks less risky and less prone to fail. A higher leverage ratio implies that the bank has to put more of its own capital relative to its debt in financing its assets (e.g. loans).
Maturity	In finance, maturity or maturity date refers to the final payment date of a loan or other financial instrument, at which point the principal (and all remaining interest) is due to be paid.
Microfinance institution (MFI)	A financial institution specialising in banking services for low-income groups or individuals.
Midcap	Mid cap is an abbreviation for the term "middle capitalisation" which is used to define the market capitalisation of a company. Market capitalisation (or market cap) is the total value of the issued shares of a publicly traded company. Traditionally, companies were divided into large-cap, mid-cap, and small-cap. There is no official definition of, or full consensus agreement about, the exact cut-off values of these indices. A rule of thumb may look like: Large-cap: Over USD 10 billion, Mid-cap: USD 2 billion – USD 10 billion, Small-cap: USD 250 million – USD 2 billion.
Non-performing loans	A Non-performing loan (NPL) is a loan that is in default or close to being in default. Many loans become non-performing after being in default for 90 days, but this can depend on the contract terms. NPLs are the value of non-performing loans divided by the total value of the loan portfolio.

(Loan) Origination	Loan origination is the process by which a borrower applies for a new loan, and a lender processes that application. Origination generally includes all the steps from taking a loan application up to disbursal of funds (or declining the application).
Private equity	In finance, private equity is an asset class consisting of equity securities and debt in operating companies that are not publicly traded on a stock exchange.
Private equity firm	A private equity firm is an investment manager that makes investments in the private equity of operating companies through a variety of loosely affiliated investment strategies, such as venture capital and growth capital.
Quota obligation	Requirement to include renewable energy in the energy mix in some capacity, such as building standards/regulations, biofuel blending, renewable energy installations in new construction, etc.
Rate of return	Rate of return is a profit on an investment over a period of time, expressed as a proportion of the original investment. The time period is typically a year, in which case the rate of return is referred to as annual return.
Return on equity	Measure of the returns earned on the owners' investment.
Security	Banking: Personal assets or property that can be pledged as collateral, also a good faith guaranty by a co-maker to pay an obligation if the borrower defaults. Finance: Certificate evidencing ownership of equity (stock). Ownership of a debt obligation payable (bond) and the right to ownership implied by options and warrants. Securities, when pledged as collateral, may be used to obtain bank financing.
Tax credit	A tax credit is a reduction of tax in order to stimulate purchasing of or investment in a certain product, like GHG emission reducing technologies.
Tax rebate	Money paid back to a person or company when they have paid too much tax.
tCO_2e	Tonnes of carbon dioxide equivalent, which is a measure that allows to compare the emissions of other greenhouse gases relative to one unit of CO_2. It is calculated by multiplying the greenhouse gas's emissions by its 100-year global warming potential.
Tenor of a loan	The length of time before a loan is due.
Venture capital (firm)	Venture capital is financial capital provided to early-stage, high-potential, growth start-up companies. The venture capital fund earns money by owning equity in the companies it invests in, which usually have a novel technology or business model in high technology industries, such as biotechnology, IT and software.
(Market) Volatility	In finance, volatility is a measure for variation of price of a financial instrument over time. Historic volatility is derived from time series of past market prices.

ORGANISATION FOR ECONOMIC CO-OPERATION AND DEVELOPMENT

The OECD is a unique forum where governments work together to address the economic, social and environmental challenges of globalisation. The OECD is also at the forefront of efforts to understand and to help governments respond to new developments and concerns, such as corporate governance, the information economy and the challenges of an ageing population. The Organisation provides a setting where governments can compare policy experiences, seek answers to common problems, identify good practice and work to co-ordinate domestic and international policies.

The OECD member countries are: Australia, Austria, Belgium, Canada, Chile, the Czech Republic, Denmark, Estonia, Finland, France, Germany, Greece, Hungary, Iceland, Ireland, Israel, Italy, Japan, Korea, Luxembourg, Mexico, the Netherlands, New Zealand, Norway, Poland, Portugal, the Slovak Republic, Slovenia, Spain, Sweden, Switzerland, Turkey, the United Kingdom and the United States. The European Union takes part in the work of the OECD.

OECD Publishing disseminates widely the results of the Organisation's statistics gathering and research on economic, social and environmental issues, as well as the conventions, guidelines and standards agreed by its members.

OECD PUBLISHING, 2, rue André-Pascal, 75775 PARIS CEDEX 16
(97 2016 02 1 P) ISBN 978-92-64-25217-2 – 2016

www.ingramcontent.com/pod-product-compliance
Lightning Source LLC
LaVergne TN
LVHW081417110826
845149LV00010B/1773
* 9 7 8 9 2 6 4 2 5 2 1 7 2 *